Potpourri of Thoughts

Uncover over 2400

Pearls of Wisdom

Murli Chari

PUSTAK MAHAL®

J-3/16 , Daryaganj, New Delhi-110002
☎ 23276539, 23272783, 23272784 • *Fax:* 011-23260518
E-mail: info@pustakmahal.com • *Website:* www.pustakmahal.com

Sales Centre

- 10-B, Netaji Subhash Marg, Daryaganj, New Delhi-110002
☎ 23268292, 23268293, 23279900 • *Fax:* 011-23280567
E-mail: rapidexdelhi@indiatimes.com
- 6686, Khari Baoli, Delhi-110006
☎ 23944314, 23911979

Branches

Bengaluru: ☎ 080-22234025 • *Telefax:* 080-22240209
E-mail: pustak@airtelmail.in • pustak@sancharnet.in
Mumbai: ☎ 022-22010941, 022-22053387
E-mail: rapidex@bom5.vsnl.net.in
Patna: ☎ 0612-3294193 • *Telefax:* 0612-2302719
E-mail: rapidexptn@rediffmail.com

ISBN 978-81-223-1373-4

Edition: 2012

Printed at : Superfine Book Binding Works, Loni (UP.)

CONTENTS

ACKNOWLEDGEMENTS

I am very much grateful to all the people I had association with specifically my family, my close friends, all the authors I have read and cherished, particularly Robin Sharma. I am especially thankful to one of my closest friends Mr. Raman, DGM in a scheduled bank who always kept supporting and inspiring me to carry on with writing and expressing my views candidly. I am grateful to my family for their unstinted support in giving valuable suggestions. I am very much grateful to the entire staff of Pustak Mahal who reposed faith in me as usually it is very difficult to find a publisher for first time writers. I am also thankful to Pustak Mahal for publishing my maiden venture "Live Life Worthwhile– 70 ways to enjoy it." I extend my gratitude to Mr. Ram Avtar Gupta, CEO, Ms Himani for helping me with the semantics, selection of thoughts and Mr. Daya Krishna for constantly following up with me in maintaining the schedule.

Last but not the least; I would like to thank Mr. Vivek Khambete, Coach & Mentor, Pune for his continuous guidance and suggestions that helped immensely in the making of this treasure chest.

ABUNDANCE

- The whole world is a buffet where you can choose as per your choice.
- World is a buffet with cornucopia of things enough for all.
- There is ample for all still we scramble for more.
- Unlimited patience and enthusiasm can get all the abundance you desire.
- Prosperity coupled with generosity is the sign of true abundance.
- Confluence of wisdom, confidence, purpose and positive attitude leads to true abundance.
- Nature's bounty is abundant but due to human avarice everything is turning out to be hell.
- There is abundance in the universe for all of us if only all of us keep aside our avarice and ego.
- Creativity and innovation in your work will enrich you abundantly.
- Let the whole world go corrupt but you remain unaffected by that as that would ensure you abundance.

ACT

- Every act should elevate you and your self-esteem.

ACTION

- Knowledge without action is of very little significance.
- Action is the best cure for fear.
- Pursuit of knowledge without action is a blunder.
- Act on your decisions to avoid lamenting later.
- Take on the fear by its horns by taking action and not be paralyzed by fear.
- Acting without thinking and thinking without acting is both fraught with disaster.
- Launch on the action on initiatives to fulfill your heart's yearning.
- Attempting something is better than just planning and not acting.
- Commiserating with others must be followed up with action.
- Take action after you have considered all the options dispassionately.
- Be an actor in your life rather than a spectator for other's performances.
- Action is the bridge between your words and deeds.
- Exuberance in action is more worthwhile than that of thoughts.
- An idea is a potential energy but only action on that will lead to its happy culmination.
- Unless we take action against injustices we will be devoured by the hooligans.
- Merely passing legislation has no meaning unless strictly implemented.

- It is better not to plan if you are not going to take action on that.
- Follow your good intentions with good act.
- Dream, think and dare to act to reach your coveted goal.
- One ounce of action is worth a ton of planning.
- No amount of advise will work unless you are prepared to take action on it.
- Action is more eloquent than words.
- Lady luck smiles on people who have the temerity to put their dreams into action.
- Unless we put our intentions into action they are merely reveries which are of no avail.
- Dreams die prematurely because we do not take ample action to realize them.
- Only daydreaming will not take you anywhere, action on that will.
- Our children learn from our actions rather than spoken advices.
- If something is bothering you, better take action or shelve it for ever.
- An ounce of action is better than tons of thinking.
- Action is an extraordinary initiative which is far better than planning coupled with inaction.
- Overcoming the inertia and taking action lends credence to your personality.
- Great actions achieve much more than great intentions without any action.

ADVENTURE

- A dash of adventure is necessary to elevate the spirits.
- Spirit of adventure multiplies your potential exponentially.
- Adventurous spirit will keep you younger for ever.
- A bold heart always looks for adventure.
- Whet your appetite for risks and adventurism and you will be amazed at your potential.

ADVERSITY

- Adversity knocks on your doors to hone your hidden faculties.
- Turn your adversities into blessing by making other's lives enjoyable.
- Treat every adversity as an opportunity to step up the ladder of success.

ADVICE

- Advise others only if you would have used the advice yourself.
- Advices are given freely but seldom accepted.
- A practical advice is worth more than all the wealth if it can help someone wriggle from a quandary.
- Paradoxically we love giving advices but we loathe to accept advices.
- To follow one's own advice is the toughest task.
- Advices must be given only when sought otherwise it is a waste of time, energy and leads to frustration.

- The amount of energy we spend in giving advice to others should be utilized for self.

AGENDA

- Have your own agenda in life lest some one thrusts his agenda on you.
- Script your own agenda as that will give you immense satisfaction and you will feel elated.
- If the human race as a whole has one single agenda of paradise on earth it will prosper in unimaginable proportions.

AIM

- Prime aim of life is to enlighten your life and that of others.

ALCOHOL

- Alcohol is a temporary solution to a permanent problem. Alcohol creates more problems than it solves.

ALONE

- It is better to be alone than to be in the shadows of others.

ALTERNATIVE

- Always keep an escape route from every situation.

ALTRUISM

- Emulate a tree which gives shade, fruits, oxygen without getting anything in return.

- Altruism is a virtue worth emulating that will make you very happy.
- Sun and nature are a paragon of altruism of the best kind.
- Make the great sun as your paradigm of altruism.
- Assure your happiness by making others happy.
- If each one of us is selfless our world will become a paradise.
- Care and concern for others will truly make you valuable and worthy.
- Make common cause with the do-gooders.
- The kind of pleasure of helping others particularly those who deserve the most but are lowly placed is unparalleled in the world.
- You will never fail if all your energies are directed towards the benefit of others.
- Pursue prosperity by all means but with a purpose to use it for the world at large.
- Looking beyond your own self-interests prepares you to receive abundance.
- Keep on showering goodness and admiration on others and the rewards will be astounding.
- Helping others with alacrity is a virtue worth developing as it benefits all and your self as well.
- Your personality will bloom if you ceaselessly endeavor to make this world a better place to live.

- When we start living for others we realize true happiness, realization of our real self and potential and god.
- Be like a sun which burns itself to give light and life to all creatures on the terra firma.
- Sky is the limit for a person who is oblivious of his own interests.
- The contributions made by so many altruistic great men is beyond imagination and we need to be grateful to them.
- Working for the good of human society as a whole needs no position of authority.

ANGER

- Anger if channelized toward constructive things will yield great results.
- Anger is a missile which boomerangs on the person who sends it.
- Anger is a cannonball that you fire at yourself.
- Anger is a double-edged knife hurting both the beholder and receiver.
- Anger makes you so mad that you will not even flinch to kill a person.
- Anger for a right cause is healthy not otherwise.
- Anger is the Achilles' heal of a person.
- Half the battle is won when we control our anger.
- Anger is momentary but has cascading effect of spoiling your entire day.

- A cantankerous person can not be trusted with weapons.
- Never allow your anger come out of the dungeon of your brain as that would play havoc.
- Channelize your anger towards right causes.
- Anger is the most inimical thing to have.
- An angry man is close to insanity.
- Never shout at others as that may snatch away your peace of mind.
- In the heat of the moment anger paralyses the rational mind.
- Insecurity and ego are at the bottom of anger.
- Trivial things coupled with anger leads to more contentious issue.
- Rein in your anger and you have won half the battle.
- Suppressing anger creates stress. You need to address this issue by replacing the anger state of mind by happy thoughts.
- Don't say or act when in a state of anger as it is one's worst enemy.
- Anger is a missile you are directing at yourself.
- Anger is your own enemy destroying your tranquility.
- Anger is counterproductive and does not serve the intended purpose.
- Anger consumes your peace of mind.
- Anger is a bug that nibbles at your peace of mind.
- Anger leaves your morale in shambles.
- We usually ventilate our anger on those who are near and dear.

- Anger most of the times boomerangs and breaches your peace of mind.

ANXIETY

- Anxiety about the result is unwarranted as that affects efforts and morale.
- Anxiety takes away the fun to attempt something riskier and adventurous. Anxiety is the number one enemy of peace.
- Anxiety and expectation leads to stress and frustration.

ARGUMENT

- Arguments avoided leads to bliss.
- An argument is squandering time on the frivolous with only heartburns.
- Argument has no rationale.
- Avoid arguments to secure peace of mind.
- Argument is futile and discussion fruitful.
- We may score a point in an argument but we may lose a good friend.
- Behind every argument there lies ego and unsatisfied heart.
- We are so keen on arguing on petty matters that we miss the big issue.
- Endless argument will end in animosity and futility.
- Needless argument leads to enmity and even grave consequences.
- The amount of time, energy and money wasted on arguments can be channelized for the greater good of all.

- Never argue with a cynic and nihilist as they will dampen your enthusiasm.

ARROGANCE

- Basking in your own glory sans arrogance boosts your confidence.
- Arrogance of man will permanently damage the heritage of nature.
- Authority without knowledge leads to arrogance.
- Mocking at others is a sure sign of superciliousness and arrogance.
- Thinking about yourself all the time is an exercise in arrogance.
- Blunders are committed due to ignorance or arrogance. More of the latter.
- We criticize, complain and condemn because we distrust others and are arrogant.
- Arrogance comes from ego and ignorance.

ATTITUDE

- Problems can either offer you bouquets or brickbats depending on your attitude.
- Trying itself is enough proof that you are not scared of failure.
- Every event will either make you better or bitter depending on your attitude.
- Failures need to be admired for they attempt to do something.

- Blaming others for everything in your life is giving up the right to live your own life.
- Success will not elude the one with 'never quit' attitude.
- Crisis will bring out the best or worst depending upon your attitude.
- Problems have the potential either to turn you into a hero or a zero depending on your attitude.
- The impact of positive attitude and thinking is tremendous.
- All the problems are psychological and can be solved by thinking positive thoughts.
- A sanguine attitude is worth your weight in gold.
- Avoiding taking risks to succeed for fear of failure and criticism is the worst attitude on your part.
- Boring moments are the result of lackadaisical attitude.
- Always be on a diet of positive attitude.
- Success may make you arrogant or humble depending upon your attitude.
- One who complains never works, one who works never complains.
- Always look at the positive things in life like a sunflower which always faces the sun.
- The energy that goes into negative attitude can rather be channelized to achieve your goals.
- With a positive attitude you can wriggle out of crisis and triumph.

AVARICE

- Our world will become a paradise if we take only what we need.
- Amassing wealth at the cost of others is a crime against humanity.
- Human society is becoming depraved by virtue of avarice.
- Garnering everything for oneself leaves one ostracized and makes one an island.
- Becoming rich by snatching others' wealth is a heinous crime.
- Avarice is the bane of human race.
- Most of our wants are basically thrust upon us by others to keep up with the Joneses.
- We are imperiling human existence by wantonly plundering nature.
- Scourge of poverty is not related to scarcity but to avarice.
- If avarice is eliminated every ill of the society can be routed out.
- A sprawling house built on the blood of poor is the most inhumane thing.
- Money and praise can arouse even a corpse.
- All the brawl is because everyone is craving to corner more without deserving.
- We keep amassing wealth for the future little sure of whether we will be there or not.
- Running after money will make you lose on life of tranquility.

- Avarice of human beings is depriving the humanity of its glory.
- Beyond meeting the basic requirements all desire is nothing but avarice.
- Live one day at a time and pour all your goodness on others.
- Only when man starts storing for the future that he commits sin to garner wealth.

BELIEF

- Self-belief is all you need to reach your goal.
- We are ready to believe the worst but never the best.
- Refuse to believe that what you aspire is impossible.
- We scarcely believe that some day we have to leave this wonderful world. If we were to, then we will mend fences with everyone.
- Believing in superstitious and ritualistic religion is not advisable as you are following without understanding.
- Believing in the words of crystal gazers is an insult to your own perceptions and understanding.
- Doubt your doubts and believe your beliefs.
- Belief in your own abilities is paramount to achieving greatness.
- Your beliefs should be sans any prejudice and judgment to be worthy.
- If you believe god and not believe yourself then that is of no use.
- Better to believe in yourself than half-heartedly believing in the almighty.

- Unless you firmly believe in something, you cannot persuade others to accept them as your body language will betray you.
- Be a fool to believe that nothing is impossible.

BIAS

- Be free of all biases to enhance your personality.
- Drain your mind of the toxins of bias against anyone and your mind will enjoy freedom and ecstasy.

BLAME

- Never blame anyone for your misfortune.
- Blaming others for your misfortune is handing over control of your life to others.

BLUNDER

- There is no blunder if one raises like the bird of phoenix.

BOOKS

- Keep company of good books to keep your morale high.
- Always keep some useful book to pass your time waiting for someone or something.
- Reading good books should be part of your daily routine.
- Books give you an advantage to enhance your horizon and understanding other perspectives.
- Right books can transform your life beyond imagination.

- No pleasure can match that of reading a good book.
- Pleasures of the senses are evanescent.
- Investing in good books by way of money, time and energy will return you thousands of times.

BOREDOM

- Boredom is the result of ignorance.
- Boredom breeds crime.
- Boredom begets inimical thoughts.
- Boredom is a sign of lack of purpose in life.
- Boredom emanates from either ennui or lack of purpose.
- Killing time to quell boredom is waste of precious life and time.
- Boredom comes to those who are lackadaisical.
- Always keep your mind busy so that boredom does not set in to breed nasty things.
- Killing boredom is easy if you think great thoughts and ideas.
- To kill boredom you need to develop interests in varied things.

BRAIN

- Clutter in the brain is worse than a clutter of garbage.
- Brain works exquisitely sans fear, anger, negativity and cynicism.

- The power of brain that we use is just a tip of the iceberg of its true potential.
- Look kills but it is the brain which thrills.
- Computers may be a miracle machine but it is still miniscule compared to the human brain.
- Brilliance of your brain is much splendid than the splendor of sun.

BRAWL

- Exchange ideas and discuss but never indulge in verbal brawl.

CALMNESS

- Being calm under any stress will fortify your personality.
- Be like an ocean with outward countenance of turbulence and inside calm. Calmness can quell any adversity.
- In a grim situation marshal all your resources and coolly think for solutions.

CATASTROPHE

- Development at the cost of ecology will prove to be catastrophic.

CAVIL

- Finding fault with others is height of cynicism and recipe for animosity.
- Don't indulge in fault finding but look for good in everybody and everything, then you will never falter.

CHANGE

- Religious practices should be revamped to correspond to the needs of time.
- Change is the most dynamic thing in the world and we need to accept it or perish.
- Change is eternal and we must tune ourselves to that lest we are in shambles.

CHARACTER

- Your character reveals your personality.
- Character is a lifeboat which saves in times of difficulty.
- Character is the bulwark in times of crisis.
- Unblemished character is worth more than all the diamonds in the world.
- Character, health and then wealth should be the priority.
- Character can make or mar a person.
- Forsake all your wealth but do not forsake character at any cost.
- The aroma of character wafts all through leaving a pleasant experience.
- Character is more valuable than reputation.
- Character is a treasure more worthier preserving and guarding than wealth.
- The philosophy of wine, dine and shine may corrode your character.
- Building character is no less than building a monument.

- Take care of your character and it will take care of everything.
- Bankruptcy of wealth is alright but bankruptcy of character is inimical.
- You cannot enslave a man of scruples.
- Indulging in carnal desires perennially may ruin your character and lead you to your nadir.
- Carry yourself with dignity and grace.
- Lacking wealth is alright but lack of character is dangerous.
- Bruises on the body is alright but not on your morality.
- Ruins of wealth may be rebuilt but not that of character.
- Your character should mirror in your behaviour .
- Power of flawless character is unfathomable.
- Worth of a man is known when he is tempted and refrains from amassing wealth stealthily while no one is watching and will not come to be detected.
- In pursuit of wealth do not compromise on character and principles as that may bring disrepute to your personality.
- Character building may bring blisters to your feet but brings joy to your feat.
- Strong character will fetch you all the things that knowledge without integrity will not do.
- It is much difficult to build character than to garner wealth.
- Character should be like a solid rock unshakeable by any impact.
- A man with character can face any blizzard and avalanche of problems.
- True character is revealed when adversity strikes.

- Character is your best friend. In times of adversity it provides succor.
- Drive away the negatives in your character and realize your dream.
- Character is to personality as spine is to body.
- Beauty is ephemeral but character is eternal.
- A strong character is vital for a good life.
- Money is both a nectar or venom depending upon the character.
- Worth of character is known only in times of crisis.
- Cheering others on their success requires strength of character.
- Character is worth your weight in gold.
- You are more worthier than the entire wealth of the world if you have an impeccable character.
- Rome was not built in a day so does building character takes time.
- If you have the character you will never shatter.
- Don't barter your character for the worldly things as that would make you worse than a prostitute who does it as a matter of necessity.
- Mortgage your property by all means but never your character and freedom.
- Character is the crowning glory for a man.
- Character leads to courage.
- Character is the bedrock on which your persona rests.
- It is easier to build a monument than character.

- A character like steel is more worthier than gold.
- Once you have built an impeccable and unimpeachable character then you have the world at your feet.
- A person of character will turn scars to stars.
- Being bereft of character is a cardinal sin worse than prostitution.
- Glamour is a superficial thing. Real glow comes from impeccable character.

CHOICE

- You are your biggest foe or friend – whatever you choose to be.
- Be choosy about what you choose.
- Present life is the cascading effect of your choices.
- Quirk of fate is nothing but the result of our own choices.
- Be careful about the choices you make as they shape your destiny.
- Bitter or better is a choice and not chance.
- Make your own choices lest you blame others.
- You have to make a choice between flourish or perish.
- Choice rather than chance will lead you to your destiny.
- Our perceptions and choices shape our destiny.
- Every action you take will take you to your destiny or away from it. So rather be careful in your choices of action.
- Too many choices complicate the matter as too little.So make a considered choice.
- One momentous choice and decision can make or mar your prospects.

- It is better to be aloof than get mired in controversy.
- One choice can lend you the right opportunity to excel. So be very deliberate in making the choice.
- There are a plethora of choices for the energetic and enthusiastic person.
- Every moment is an opportunity to turn itself into a magic or tragic one. Choice is entirely ours.
- You are as free as your choice provided it is not crossing other's paths.
- Your life is a manifestations of the choices you have made.
- Plenty of choices has made taking a decision a herculean task.
- The choice of friends and books decide your destiny.
- Worry kills and cheerfulness thrills.
- Demon and divine both are in you. It is your destiny to discover the divine.
- Money is divine or satanic depending upon what you spend.
- The choices you make in life will shape your destiny.
- We have choices either to adopt, change or shift to different situations instead of cribbing.
- Tread on your own chosen path as you know yourself best.
- Live life as per your own choices rather than that of others as you are your best judge.

CIRCUMSTANCES

- Circumstances impel but not compel.

COMMERCIALIZATION

- Too much of commercialization has rendered man the commodity.
- Crass commercialization has snatched the soul from the society.
- Too much commercialization has demeaned the sanctity of human relationships.
- Crass commercialization has rendered human beings into a commodity with a price tag.
- Commercialization has marauded humanity and character, which are more vital than anything else.
- Too much of commerce is spoiling the harmony of nature, human beings and society.
- Commerce has taken a heavy toll on ethics and humanity.
- Too much of commercialization makes every body a commodity in the market.
- Commercialization brings the best of mind and the worst of heart.
- Crass commercialization has rendered human beings to greedy species little realizing the endowments of human beings.

COMPANY

- Being alone is better than bad company.
- Even if you feel low hobnob with the great people.
- Company of oneself should also be comfortable to you lest you are not happy with yourself.

COMPETITION

- Competition drains your energy and creates foes.
- Unethical competition should be avoided to do away with attrition of humanity.

COMPLAINT

- Never complain as that might bring misfortune.
- To express whimper if things are not going your way you are heading for despondency.

CONCEIT

- Bragging about oneself is conceit.
- Blowing your own trumpet gets you no accolades.
- Argument emanates from conceit.
- Even inveterate criminal will not accept that he is wrong as every one stoutly defends his position.

CONCENTRATION

- Momentary lapse of concentration is the reason for many calamities.
- Be aware, agile and alert as even a momentary lapse of concentration can cost you heavily.

CONSCIENCE

- Your conscience is the mirror which will reflect your true self.

- Clear conscience is a great attribute that will keep you in perpetual bliss.
- Communication with your conscience can save you from many heartburns.
- A clear conscience is the best tranquilizer.
- Having qualms of conscience for inhuman things is the sign of greatness.
- To transgress your own conscience is the worst blight on your character.
- Clear conscience is a beacon guiding you in tough times.
- Listening to your inner voice will keep you away from doing evil things.
- You may remove the evidences but the vestiges of your crime lingers on in your conscience.
- Breaching your conscience is rocking the very boat you are riding.
- A litany of sins will make you bereft of qualms of conscience and make you imbecile.
- Conscience is the first casualty when you commit a sin.
- A fugitive may run away but his conscience will keep pricking.
- Conscience is the cauldron where every thing has to be tested.
- Conscience is your mirror which reflects as you are.
- If you listen to the dictates of your conscience than you need no rules to follow.
- Guilt-ridden conscience will nibble at your peace of mind.

- A crystal clear conscience is the mark of a great man.
- Listening to the dictates of your conscience will keep you on track.
- Wrong doings will nibble at your conscience and will make you restless.

CONTROL

- Keeping your tongue under leash is far better than keeping your purse under leash.
- Reining in your emotions is worth its attempt and rewarding.
- Control of your life depends on the thoughts you think and choices you make.
- No body has any control over what you think, decide and act.
- Don't hand over the control of your life to others as that is a recipe for failure.
- Let the mind work faster than your tongue as unbridled tongue can land you in a soup.
- Rein in your anger and tongue and you will be happy.
- Having control over your thoughts will provide you control over your life.

COOPERATION

- Cooperation is an elixir boosting amity.
- Together we can flourish but each one to oneself is sure to perish.

- In recent times we have become competitive instead of being cooperative to serve everyone's purpose.
- Compete with yourself and cooperate with others.

CORRUPTION

- Corruption is more lethal than murder.
- Corruption is killing people on a daily basis.
- Corruption is vitiating the humanity within and without.
- Corruption is at the root of all the ills of the society.
- Corruption is the worst foe of humanity.
- Corruption is nothing but a sophisticated form of killing people.

COURAGE

- An intrepid person will take on any problem. Your fears are straw monsters if you boldly challenge them.
- Never let fear paralyze you, rather take it by its horns.
- Laughing at one's foibles needs great courage.
- Courage in times of crisis is more valuable than abundance of wealth coupled with cowardice.
- Courage is the most formidable virtue.
- Light the lamps of courage to drive away the ghost of fear.
- To be an atheist requires formidable courage.
- Indomitable courage can take on the Goliath of evil-mongers.

- All virtues are in vain if one lacks courage.
- Sang-froid in the face of danger is true courage.
- Look at yourself with trepidation for the colossal courage you possess.
- Have the courage to admit your blunders and correct them as that would make you a great person.
- Decrepit people are scared of even the mole and intrepid are not scared of even the mountain.
- Most of the fears are imaginative and unfounded .
- If we dare, many things fall in place.
- Laughing at one's gaffe requires courage and humility.
- Allowing space to others to transform themselves requires courage.
- Toughness of mind can withstand physical pain gracefully.
- Quell all the fear and act boldly.
- For want of courage we indulge in back-biting which is not in good taste.
- Don't shy away from fear rather take it by the horns and trample it.
- Put up a brave face even in adversity and you will come out unscathed.
- Having indomitable courage is what separates the great from the ordinary.
- Faith in self and others requires indomitable courage.
- Think boldly and act fearlessly.
- Never panic even in times of danger as it further complicates the matter.

- We should always remain unruffled and nonchalant in times of dire situations.
- Challenge every fear and you will become courageous and achieve anything.
- Build courage bit by bit by conquering fear that emanates from your mind.
- Force yourself to be courageous and confident and you will have won half the battle.
- Ordinary people manifest exemplary courage in combating adversities.

COURTESY

- Be courteous to all as everyone has self-worth.
- A candid opinion need not be discourteous.

CRIME

- Deriving pleasure out of pain to others is cannibalism. Educated people committing crime is most unpardonable.
- Most crimes emanate from lust, hatred, anger and jealousy.
- Genocide in the name of religion and patriotism is the worst crime against humanity.
- Most of the crimes are due to envy, greed and lust.
- Ravaging the modesty of a women is the worst crime in the world.
- Leaving anyone in the lurch is a horrendous crime.
- Don't be even a tacit accomplice in evil-mongering as that would make you part of the crime.
- Even sinister planning sans action is a crime of the worst kind.

CRISIS

- Your true nature is manifested in times of crisis.
- Every crisis is an inferno in which you purify your personality and rid yourself of wastes.
- Every crisis is an opportunity to prop up your strength.
- Tsunami of crisis strikes those who have no vision and priorities.
- Crisis tests your character, attitude and patience.

CRITIC

- Be your own critic and connoisseur to avoid outside interference.
- Be your own critic and impassionate judge and you will rise to greatness.

CRITICISM

- Do not fire a barrage of criticism as that may boomerang.
- Criticism should be removed from the lexicon of society and replaced with appreciation to reap the harvest.
- Criticism is a bitter pill to cure the disease.
- Never ever criticize others as that would shatter them.
- Criticism kills the enthusiasm.
- Accept criticism as a compliment or you will feel flustered.
- Criticism is lethal fraught with inimical implications.
- Every criticism impairs both the giver and the receiver.

- If we can digest criticism then we can be very composed.
- However logical your criticism is it is bound to reflect criticism towards you.
- Criticism is a double-edged knife which cuts both ways.
- There is a virtual orgy of criticism in the world.
- Behind every criticism is the desire to prove one's smartness.

CURIOSITY

- A curious brain is the key to abundance of knowledge.
- There is no ennui for an inquisitive mind.
- Have an unsatiating curiosity to learn new things.
- Curiosity is enough to garner all the education, knowledge and wisdom.
- No knowledge can remain locked against the power of curiosity.
- Imbibe the abundant innocence and curiosity of children and you will be richly rewarded and enriched.
- Curiosity will reward generously rather than rote.
- Curiosity is the sure shot key to acquiring knowledge.
- Sow the seeds of curiosity in children and they will pursue knowledge on their own without the formal stereo-type education.

CYNIC

- Cynic is a sadist seeking failure in everything.
- Being skeptical about everything is being a cynic.
- Cynic will degrade every brilliant idea even before giving it a fair chance to succeed.

CYNICISM

- Cynicism is the recipe for disaster.
- Cynicism is a graveyard which buries you even before you die.

DARE

- Dare to blaze the trail breaking all traditions.
- Don't keep complaining about lack of opportunity but dare to seize them.
- One who dares never cares and one who cares never dares.

DEED

- The pleasure one gets from good deeds is invaluable and better than carnal pleasures.

DEMEANOR

- Have the gumption to fight adversities with a happy demeanor.
- You can unlock any door if you have a smile on your face and humility in your heart.
- Don't repel others by your demeanor.

DESIRE

- Strong and genuine desires are always rewarded.
- Ravenous desire leads you to your nemesis.
- Unsatiated desires leaves you flustered.

- Rejoice and be grateful for what you have and you will have more of what you desire.
- Desires themselves will not yield results unless commitment and purpose is there.

DESTINY

- Keep fate out of the gate. Reliance on fate is surrendering your life to the vagaries of events.
- Be selective about what you read, listen and see as that would shape your destiny.
- Our tryst with destiny will dawn when every one is transformed into real human beings.
- Repel negative people and thoughts to have sway over your destiny.
- Every person has to take his own route to attain his density but that should benefit others for it to be successful.

DISAPPOINTMENT

- Euphoria and melancholy should be brief lest it ends in disappointment.

DISCERN

- Discern the words of the wise and that of a fool.
- Sift the wisdom from information to remove the clutter to provide clarity of thoughts.

DISCOVERY

- Discovering oneself is the greatest accomplishment and reward.

DISCUSSION

- Discussion leads to results and argument to malice.
- All matters must be thoroughly discussed, decided and done.

DISDAIN

- Don't look at anyone with disdain as that may boomerang.

DISPOSITION

- A cheerful disposition lends you a good social position.
- Belligerent disposition is an invitation to trouble.

DISTORTION

- Killing in the name of religion is tantamount to tarnishing the precepts of god.

DOUBT

- Doubts and fears are the greatest impediment to success.
- Deeper and deeper you delve into yourself more you discover yourself which is infinite.
- Once you have discovered yourself you have discovered the world.

DREAM

- Dream is the clay to mould your life.
- Dream the ultimate life and put everything into your efforts.
- Keep dreaming on a daily basis and shun regrets.
- Don't drown yourself in the deluge of regrets rather focus on dreams.
- Regrets do not help you to mend the past whereas dreams provide momentum to brighten your future.
- Extreme dreams are a possibility if you believe and are ready to pay the price.
- Be honest to your dreams however much people laugh, ridicule and criticize you.
- Wishful thinking can provide the right fillip to realize your dreams.
- Fountain of youth will continue if you keep dreaming.
- If your dreams are genuine and in the interest of all you will find all the resources and energy.
- Your dreams are supreme to you. Don't expect others to nourish it as they may not understand the depth of it and nurse envy.
- Realize the potential of your dreams and you will feel elated.
- It costs nothing to stretch you dreams to the extreme but it costs dearly not to do that.
- Keep alive the dreams you had in your youth as they can be realized irrespective of your age.
- You might have miserably failed but have your dreams intact then you are still on way to success.

- Dreams while awake has more potential than dreams while sleeping.
- Dare to dream and fulfill with full steam.
- Fulfilling the dreams of others will get you to your dream.
- Dreams in day light is more useful than dreams during sleep.
- Keep on dreaming and keep on nourishing them and you will reach great heights.
- Keep dreaming and you will never get old.
- Dreams magnetize your personality and you can realize your cherished goals.
- You have to nourish your dream and flourish. So don't depend on others to fulfill your dreams.

DRUDGERY

- You must loaf around sometimes to take away the drudgery of routine things.
- Education and work needs to be rid of drudgery to be more beneficial and meaningful.

EDUCATION

- Every person should have his syllabus of education rather than yielding to the conventional.
- The education system has snatched the natural curiosity of the students.
- All education is worthless sans humility and grace.
- Studying to get degrees is worthless unless used for the good of all.

- Illiteracy spells doom and education liberates.
- Education frees human beings from all the tyranny.
- Formal education is too regimented to allow for mistakes which make one learn better.
- True education liberates one from biases.
- If education cannot liberate it is of no avail.
- Education is the most beautiful investment which provides you with freedom from poverty, stress and also enlightenment.
- Law enforcers should educate people to refrain from committing crimes rather than catching them after commitment of crime.
- Present day education is taking away the innocence and fun of children.
- Travel and adoption of others' culture is the best way to acquire education and develop relationships.
- Be on a continuous education from various sources like good books, internet, television, radio, from really successful people and your own and others' experiences.
- Life's purpose is to learn and act accordingly.
- Denying the privilege of education to the desolate is inimical to all.
- True education leads to true greatness beyond imagination.
- Education needs to be imparted free or at reasonable cost so that even the poorest can afford and everyone can realize their full potential.

EGO

- Ego is an unruly horse which may topple you anytime.
- Drown your ego to burgeon your knowledge and respect.
- Ego is the greatest hurdle in the pursuit of wisdom.
- We are on the threshold of a beautiful planet if everyone puts aside his ego.
- To be an egotist is inimical to true happiness.
- Set aside your ego and everything will come flowing to you.
- Intoxication of wine is far better than intoxication due to ego.
- Ego is more fragile than a glass as it can break any time.
- Ego keeps you incarcerated in your own dungeon.
- Unbridled ego is one of the worst sins and inimical to your growth.
- Having a bloated ego is a sure-shot sign of megalomania.
- Ego is the worst impediment in course to knowledge and relationship.
- A bloated ego is the unbecoming of a man.
- Ego is born out of arrogance and ignorance.
- Egos clash but humility bonds.
- Your ego will lead you astray as it is your worst enemy.
- Human ego has divided the society into fissiparous people.
- Be flexible and you will gain a lot as rigidity is born out of ego.
- Losing your ego will lead to winning over others.

- Let not laurels bloat your ego as you are blocking many more laurels to come.
- Winning an argument at any cost is the worst folly as it is guided by ego rather than love.
- Pandering to your ego-needs, is very inimical to your personality.
- Always waiting to score a point is a sign of bloated ego.
- Wisdom eludes many learned people because of their bloated ego.
- Even the lowliest of person has his own ego in spite of his humble position.
- Even a semblance of ego will make you a villain.
- Ego conflicts give rise only to enmity and bad blood.
- Keep aside ego and you will find that we are woven together in a single fabric called the universe.
- A man's ego is the barricade to real happiness.
- Ego is the worst hurdle for acquiring knowledge as it feels it knows everything and it is below dignity to accept that.
- We stay glued to a small strip of land without realizing the whole planet is ours.
- Ego is the greatest hurdle on the road to success.
- If all keep aside their ego and come together paradise can be created on earth.
- Ego keeps you away from true knowledge and pleasure.
- Ego makes you revolve around yourself and lose valuable things.
- While accepting a challenge don't make it an ego issue.

- Ego is a speed breaker which cuts the flow and speed of everything viz. knowledge, love and wisdom.
- Ego is a quagmire which drowns us and makes us miserable.
- We raise the walls in relationships by listening to our egos.
- Ego drives you to nowhere and humility to paradise.

EMOTION

- A person bereft of emotions is an animal.
- Don't be a victim of swaying emotions.
- Bereft of emotion bereft of soul.
- A workman emotionally involved in a work will do wonders rather than by only using his mind.
- The more you fret and fume the more you get frustrated.
- Don't be blinded by emotion rather think calmly.
- Emotion leads to commotion as it has no rationale.
- Take away emotions from your life and you become a cadaver.

EMULATION

- Marveling at others is no doubt good but will be best if you emulate them.
- We keep admiring and rejoicing in the qualities of great men but pay very little attention to emulating them ourselves.
- It is far better to emulate the greats than merely extolling their virtues.

- Extolling the virtues of great will be of no use unless you practice it yourself.

ENCOURAGEMENT

- Keep encouraging yourself and others to grow together. Encouragement boosts the morale and criticism impairs it.
- Many people shelve their dreams for want of encouragement.

ENTHUSIASM

- Enthusiasm compensates for lack of skill and knowledge.
- Enthusiasm is the spirit of a person.
- Joy and enthusiasm are the panacea for every problem.
- Boundless joy and enthusiasm can achieve anything.
- Enthusiasm is a nuclear power in action.
- Bubbling enthusiasm is the panacea for success.
- Boundless enthusiasm is the key to joy in doing any work.
- Enthusiasm provides you unlimited tranche of energy.
- Fill your life with enthusiasm and love and you will have no regrets.
- Enthusiasm makes any work enjoyable and is stress-free.
- Unbridled enthusiasm is better than inaction.
- Lack of money, skill and ability is often not the cause but lack of enthusiasm for trying great things is.
- Enthusiasm transforms you into a bundle of energy.

- Enthusiasm gives the energy to commit ourselves to even a difficult task.
- Enthusiasm is a magic wand which can create miracles.
- Act with gusto and without expectation and you will attain bliss.
- Enthusiasm will make your work enjoyable and rewarding.
- Enthusiasm gives you phenomenal energy to tackle even the most difficult things with joy.
- Enthusiasm coupled with positive emotions will bring immense rewards.
- Enthusiasm is a lubricant which smoothens and improves efficiency.
- Lacking in enthusiasm is far worse than lack of skills.
- With enthusiasm you can progress with leaps and bounds even though you may lack other skills.
- Joy and enthusiasm embellishes your life.
- Enthusiasm is such a dynamo power that lack of all else is also not a deterrent.
- Enthusiasm is the most dominant factor responsible for success in any endeavour.
- Enthusiasm impels you to move ahead full steam and makes the job enjoyable.

ETHICS

- Pursuit of wealth sans ethics is debauchery.
- Education sans ethics is fraught with danger.

- Pursuit of money resorting to unethical means is a horrendous crime against human society.
- Desire for money must be tempered with ethical values.
- Amassing wealth in an unethical manner is a crime against humanity.
- Adhering to ethics even in times of adversity is the true test of character and aplomb.
- Business without ethics is prostitution.
- However rapid strides the technology makes and the world becomes modern, basic ethics are a must for the society to survive.
- Education without ethics is licking honey tinkered with cyanide.
- Unethical practices to earn wealth will make you lecherous.

EVOLUTION

- We have the rich heritage of millions of years of evolution.
- Involve yourself in all good things so that you evolve as a truly great human being.
- Be grateful to nature which has taken billions of years to evolve you to your present state.
- Evolving every moment requires love, patience and understanding.
- It has taken eons for man to evolve to his present stature.
- Women are the very epitome of mother earth.
- The effort that has gone into evolving into present stage of human beings is colossus but we spend time ruing what we lack.

- Millions of years of evolution has put the human race in its present state. Why not capitalize that?

EXCUSE

- Excuses are many but one reason is enough to do anything.
- Impossible is just an excuse for not taking bold initiatives.

EXHIBITIONISM

- Profligacy and brandishing in the glare of a starved person is inviting disaster.

EXPECTATION

- Expectations from near and dear ones will make you flustered.
- Expectation leads to frustration.
- Expectation of a result leaves you flustered and anxious.
- Expecting others to bail you out of your crisis will lead to frustration.
- Expectation of something from every relationship is the greatest hurdle in being rewarded.
- Remove expectation from your lexicon and you will always remain in a state of bliss.
- Do the best things you can sans anxiety of expectation and you will be richly rewarded.
- Never put up with the ordinary and always insist the best from yourself and others. You will be surprised to receive the best.

- All our endeavors will fructify if fully focused on the job at hand without expectation of the result.
- Living up to your own expectations is true measure of character and resolve.
- Think that the worst is over and the best is yet to come.
- The problem with expecting is anxiety and frustration.

FAILURE

- Don't give up in spite of series of failures as ultimately you will succeed. Take every failure in your stride as destiny belongs to you.
- Odyssey of failures lead to true success.
- The odyssey of failures is the route to success.
- Every failure can play havoc or magic on how you perceive.
- You are a failure only when you give up and relinquish your initiative.
- Failures should be complimented so that they make more attempts to succeed.
- Going through failures prepares you for success and fortifies your personality.
- A galore of failures is worthy if you never give up in terms of lessons and success.
- Failure sculpts your personality to proceed further towards your goal.
- Never accept failure before trying once again.
- Failure is not final as long as you never give up on your efforts in the direction of your goals.

- Looking for lame excuses to explain your failure is accepting defeat instead of showing resilience.
- Failure can teach better lessons than success.
- Failure does not remain a failure unless you stop moving further.
- Failures are the ladder to climb to the acme of success.
- Failures are not cardinal sins as they carve out a niche for you as you will succeed ultimately.

FATE

- You start blaming fate when you give up trying.
- Reliance on fate will lead you to shambles.
- Don't resign to fate as it is treacherous to one self.
- There is no point in cursing your fate for all your problems.
- It is better to take action to find solutions to them.
- You may have thousand reasons to resign to your fate but find one reason to circumvent your circumstances as you are unique.
- Over reliance on fate to deliver the miracle is like fishing in a dry lake.
- Flirting with fate is like expecting crop without sowing.
- We are so quick to resign to fate that we surrender even before we have embarked on the journey.
- There is no cruelty of fate. It is all the manipulations of the villains of humanity. Resigning to fate is surrendering your initiatives to the uncertainties of nature.

- The hackneyed phrase of everything happens for good is a myth as we are surrendering everything to chance.
- Depending on fluke and fortune to deliver you from your miseries is one of the worst choices.
- Fortune favours the brave because he takes massive initiative and not due to fate.
- Fate is a word in the lexicon of cowards.
- Relying on fortune to salvage your life is living in a fool's paradise.
- Lamenting about fate is a colossal waste of time. Rather focus all your energy on what you want.
- Fortunes fluctuate when you resign to your fate rather than choosing your action.
- Risking everything on the fate to deliver is diving into the river without knowing swimming.
- Quirk of fate is all bullshit since the results are either due to your lack of commitment or manipulations of other people.
- Never complain about your fate as you can change it the way you want.
- Cursing your fate will make your life more miserable rather make choices and take action to elevate your status.
- Fate is a convenient philosophy for those who are scared of trying enough.
- Celestial stars have no role in your life.
- Comedy can turn to tragedy and tragedy can turn to comedy by quirk of fate.
- Constellation of stars cannot decide your fate as that depends upon your intention and commitment.

FEAR

- Don't grope in the dark on the crutches of fear and doubt.
- Fear may paralyze you and put your life in shambles.
- Drive the ghost of fear away to succeed.
- Allay all the fears and doubts to enrich life.
- The more you fear about fear the more it will make you frightened.
- Fear will always leave you in the lurch and will make you grope in the dark.
- Fears are your worst foes and courage your best ally.
- Fear the fear as fear may paralyze your mind and you will commit blunders, consequences of which are quite avoidable.
- If you do not foray into something for fear of failure, ridicule, and criticism you are working against your own interest.
- Never be scared of death as you will never live life fully with that thought.
- Insecurity and fear makes people behave in a foolish way.
- Cowardly approach takes away the fun from life.
- Logic takes backseat when fear paralyses the mind.
- If you are scared of thorns then never think of plucking the roses.
- Fear of the unknown paralyses your rational thinking.
- Most of the times we imagine the worst which never occur.
- We often imagine the worst but it turns out to be a straw monster.
- Fear is a monster which needs to be brutally killed to allow one to grow.

- Conquer fear by taking it by horns.
- Remove fear from your life and add courage to your character and you will have harnessed your vast potential.
- Crush the fear with a heavy hand as that destroys your morale and shakes your confidence.
- Fear is a ghost which devours your confidence.
- Act boldly and the ghost will flee.
- Fear is a dracula sucking your energy and motivation.
- Fear of failure is more fearful than failure itself.

FELICITY

- Do everything with felicity as any effort will take away the grace.

FLOW

- Keep flowing with the natural flow but keep a vigil on where you are going.
- Flow of unbridled imagination and thoughts is very refreshing.
- Don't let flow of events to drag you involuntarily.

FORGIVENESS

- Forgiveness is a divine virtue assuring you of ultimate bliss.
- Forgiveness is a virtue worth developing as it can put you in a state of bliss.
- Quality of forgiveness is the most coveted one to live in peace.

- Instead of taking revenge, forgive the person which would be more humiliating and transforming for your adversary.
- You should pardon others on their mistakes and guide them to better life.
- Keep on forgiving people for their wrong demeanors and they will be transformed.

FREEDOM

- Freedom from all biases makes a man great.
- Abuse of freedom to affect the freedom of others is criminal.
- Freedom to do anything is alright only when you do not infringe on the freedom of others.
- Freedom means responsibility and not the absence of it.
- Remaining stoical gives you the freedom to enjoy every event good or bad.
- Every child can be precocious if left to himself/herself.
- You will do wonders if you are given the freedom to do what you hold dear to your heart.
- Freedom of thoughts is much more valuable than freedom from want.
- Seeking freedom requires irresolute courage and responsibility.
- Do not encroach upon the freedom of others as that would create bad blood.
- Freedom has no meaning for those struggling for an existence.
- You can release the bird of freedom if you break the cage of negativity.

- Freedom from ignorance will lead to all freedoms.
- When you dedicate your life to humanity then you have real freedom.
- We need to break the shackles of the past to ride into a bright future.
- Freedom is not a license to trample upon the freedom of others.
- You can enslave the body but you cannot enslave the soul of a true human being.

FRIEND

- A book is the greatest friend of man.
- We should rather be like friends with one and all in spite of age considerations.
- Only a true friend, will tell you your shortcomings and greatness with honesty.
- A friend will never rationalize when he is sympathizing with you.
- A crisis is when pretenders leave you and a real friend walks in.
- Your true friends will never desert you in times of crisis and flatter you when you are prospering.
- Turn every adversity and adversary into your friend to take full advantage.
- Never ever forget your friends when you achieve success which may desert you anytime and not your true friends.

- No body is going to give you testimony unless he is a true friend of yours.
- Befriend yourself to lead a happy life.
- One good friend is worth the world.
- Make good books and the wise, your true friends to set new trends.

FRIENDSHIP

- Friendship is tested in times of adversity as you would find many in times of prosperity.
- True friends are those who sail with you in the boat of crisis.
- Friendship is not merely partying, dining and wining together but the pall bearers of trials and triumphs.
- Friendship is a parachute which will always ensure safe landing in times of crisis.
- Friendship is to provide succor even before being asked.
- Relatives demand everything as a matter of right but a friend may never compel you to part with.
- At least have one friend who totally relies on you blindly.
- Look upon others as friends and not as objects to be exploited.
- Friendship is a tree which gives fruits, shade, leaves and oxygen without expecting anything in return.
- Nourishing friendship requires lot of sacrifice, pain, love and understanding.

- Real friendship is tested in times of crisis and not when the going is good.
- Friendship requires commitment, nurturing and renewing of relationship from both the sides.
- True friendship is an oasis in the desert.
- Value friendship more than your wealth.
- Build a strong network of friendship and you have built a paradise.
- Friendship is like a banana tree whose every part is of immense value.

FROWN

- Frowning upon others is inflicting injury on self. Frowning on others will boomerang on you.
- Man with a frown can never wear a crown.

GENERATION

- Dynamism of the youth and the wisdom of the old needs to be blended for accomplishment of a salubrious human society.
- If we don't adapt to the new environs we will face cultural shock and always be at loggerheads with the younger generation.

GENEROSITY

- Generosity is a virtue which will richly reward you.
- Be generous with your wealth and knowledge.

- Be generous with the poor and stingy with the rich.
- Be generous with wealth, knowledge and happiness and stingy with criticism and negativity.
- Don't be generous with an intention to receive accolades as that will not give you true happiness.
- Generosity without expectation of reward will lead to rich rewards.
- Generosity is an insurance against adversities, as they come back in droves.
- Shower your generosity on the have not and there will be an avalanche of happiness and abundance.
- Generosity with an eye on accolades and admiration takes away the fun from it.
- Generosity begets abundance.
- Generosity is an insurance for prosperity.
- Wealth spent in promoting wisdom, knowledge and humanity is well spent.

GENOCIDE

- Daylight robbery by the politicians is akin to genocide.
- Genocide in the name of patriotism and religion is the worst crime against humanity.

GIFT

- Healthy body and mind is an indomitable gift.
- Gift of wisdom is far better than any other gift.
- We seldom realize the importance of something till we lose it.

- You can turn every situation into a gift of better or bitter you.
- Ability to think, plan and act is a tremendous blend of virtues endowed to human beings.
- Human beings are endowed with so much of gift but we squander our lives on frivolous issues.
- If we are to pay the price for our gifts of body and mind it will run into billions of dollars.
- Trillions of cells coordinate to take one action but we take everything for granted.
- If you really understand the gift of life you will become restless in acquiring wisdom and lending help to others.
- Your endowments are so precious that you realize it only when you lose them.
- Life is a rare gift which should not be squandered on mundane things.
- Treat every happening as a divine gift from nature and proceed towards your destiny.

GLAMOUR

- Glamour has no intrinsic worth.
- Glamour has limited time span of sheen and then it withers away.
- Superficial glamour loses its sheen as soon as you express yourself.

GOAL

- Every choice and every moment should take you to your goal.

- Take the good and the bad in your stride and keep marching ahead towards your coveted goal.
- If you have a definite purpose and a burning desire you will find resources to achieve your goal.
- In pursuit of your goals be sure not to hurt others.
- Ceaselessly pursue your goal even in the face of adversity.
- In pursuit of your goal do not hurt the feelings of people you meet along.
- Breaking goals into small sizes which are achievable during a day does not look daunting.
- A dash of enthusiasm, a bushel of positive attitude, a modicum of confidence and abounding action can go a long way in achieving your goals.

GOODNESS

- Be the avant-garde for good things.
- Doing good to others rewards one immensely.
- The semblance of good that we see today is due to the unassuming and altruistic few.
- Keep looking, hearing and speaking good things, you are assured of heaven.

GOOD-THINGS

- Keep company of good people, good thoughts and good books.
- Add fertilizer to good things to nourish good and weed out the evil.
- Have a panache for good things and forget the naysayers.

GOSSIP

- Beware of the gossip-mongers as they lead you to disaster.

GRACE

- Grace in everything will bring sophistication to your personality. Grace is a virtue which adorns a man.
- Grace under any circumstance is the sign of greatness.
- Very few are endowed with grace in spite of their education and wealth.
- Grace is a rare virtue which adorns one's personality.
- Be graceful in all facets of life as that is a rare virtue.
- Avoid making snide remarks on anyone in the public as it will put you to disgrace.
- Carrying yourself with grace and dignity even in an embarrassing situation is a jewel in your crown.
- Aging gracefully requires wisdom and deep understanding of life.
- If women were to behave like men then the grace of feminism is lost.
- Flaunting one's ego, wealth and knowledge is lack of grace and humility.

GRATEFULNESS

- Man should be grateful for the cornucopia of gifts bestowed by nature.
- We must thank all the people who have given us the bountiful life.

- Gratefulness and forgiveness can rid human society from rancor and odium.
- If you are gorgeous, you need to be grateful to nature and need not be too haughty about that.
- Think of all the things available to us through nature and great men that we should be happy but we grieve for what we do not have.
- Ever be grateful to people who stood by you in your bad times.
- Gratefulness is an insurance for future favours.
- When you rise in the morning thank the divine for one more day full of opportunities and when you go to bed be grateful that you are alive.
- We must thank all the people who have given us the **bountiful** life.
- Think of all the things available to us through nature and great men that we should be happy about. Don't grieve for what we do not have.

GREATNESS

- Keep fooling yourself you are great and you will become one.
- Be your own connoisseur to raise yourself to the acme of greatness.
- A truly great man will never despise others.
- Freedom from bias is rudimental to true greatness.
- Turn every moment into a great one and you will be great.
- Choose to do great things daily as that will make you happy,

boost your confidence and make your life purposeful.

- Kindness of heart and humility of mind is the key to true greatness.
- Looking forward to doing great things everyday is a great thing to do first thing in the morning.
- Grace, generosity and goodness blend to make you great.
- Sangfroid is the hall mark of true greatness.
- Respect for the culture, tradition and religion of others is a sign of true greatness.
- Heart of gold, mind of diamond and body of steel makes a person great.
- All the great men had humility, compassion and determination to leave their legacy.
- All great men are both simple and enigmatic.
- When you become great be unmindful of the remarks of critics and cynics.
- Evil-mongers are their own worst enemy as they are oblivious of the great feeling of being a good Samaritan.
- Greatness is not the exclusive preserve of the great as even common men can also be great in their own way.
- Be a parable of virtue, wisdom and generosity.
- Greatness should be coupled with humility, love and selfless service.
- Every human being is great if he explores within himself and shuns negativity.

- Humility of the mind and love-filled heart makes a man great.
- Weaving your life around principles, values and character is true greatness.
- Be a no limit person by taking on great work to make this world a better place.

HAGGLE

- We spend more time haggling for a few bucks spoiling our time, energy and respect.

HAPPINESS

- A happy demeanor will take on the goliath of insurmountable problem.
- Be the harbinger of love and happiness.
- Happiness is a choice.
- Treat everyone as a divine being and you will have all the happiness.
- After every suffering ensues happiness.
- Happiness is a state of mind and does not depend on the outside world.
- True happiness comes from a timely help to a stranger.
- Happiness comes effortlessly but eludes you if you make an effort.
- Happiness even in the face of adversity is true greatness.
- Lasting happiness comes when we make others happy.

- Pursuit of happiness is far better than pursuit of wealth.
- The attributes of wonder and excitement will keep you happy and lively.
- We must rejoice the success of others and we will have ample of opportunities to be happy.
- The more you depend on outside world for your happiness the more you will feel miserable.
- Smile as much as possible, laugh as much as possible and cry as little as possible to be happy.
- You will be extremely happy if you choose to be so.
- Rejoice in others' success as well and you will have all the reasons to be happy eternally.
- Never confine yourself to pursuit of your own happiness and you will be abundantly happy.
- Sing while you work and you will not experience monotony.
- Spreading happiness will bring you abundant happiness.
- Probe deep into yourself and you will find all the happiness ensconced within your self.
- Make everyone your friend to ensure happiness.
- Evil mongers are unfortunate in the sense that they have not derived the happiness that comes from being good.
- We should not depend upon the worldly things for happiness as happiness is within us in immense measure.
- If you desire perennial happiness, turn inwards.
- Knowledge of the world will give you immense riches but knowledge of self will reward you imperishable happiness.

- Happiness is inversely proportional to expectations.
- Keeping aloof from all vices and evils will ensure happiness.
- Happiness even under dire circumstances will make you a great person.
- Happiness is like water which squeezes out when you try to hold it and flows if let free.

HATRED

- Hatred is an inferno in which you burn yourself without affecting the hated.
- Don't nurture hatred as everything is evanescent.
- Hatred is an inferno disturbing your tranquil as it is your own enemy.
- Hatred is a poison we are dissolving in our system.
- Hatred precipitates the matter for the beholder rather than the hated.

HEALTH

- Health without wealth is better than wealth without health.
- You can be healthy without being wealthy but you cannot be wealthy without being healthy.
- Take care of your health, health will take you to great heights.

HELP

- A modicum of help in times of crisis is worth more than a ton of advice.

- Timely help is bigger than the biggest mountain.
- An ounce of help is better than tons of advice.
- Look for ways to help others as that will give you immense peace and happiness.
- Look for opportunities to lend your helping hand to those who are in distress and that will give you eternal bliss.
- Always accept and provide help in times of need.
- A lie or two to save someone is absolutely fine.
- We rush to help who are strong rather than the underprivileged though they deserve the most.
- You will flourish if you help others achieve their dreams and will perish if you trample upon others'.
- Provide help to those in need and you will enrich yourself on the way.
- We are at our best when we are helping others and at our worst when helping oneself in a selfish manner.
- The greatest help you can lend to others is to refrain from dabbling in their affairs.
- The joy of helping a rank stranger gives ultimate pleasure which words cannot describe.
- Best way to help yourself is to help others.
- A timely help is better than tons of advice.

HONESTY

- Honesty may not pay any material rewards but will keep you and your conscience happy.

- Honesty needs to be cherished and rewarded in these days of rank opportunism.
- Humanity can sustain if honesty is recognized and rewarded.
- Pursuing honesty with the intention to seek rewards is a recipe for frustration as it does not assure you any mental satisfaction.
- In these times of humongous corruption honesty makes a sensational news.
- In these days of rampant corruption we need to award honesty which is rather a prerequisite to a healthy society.

HOPE

- Hope is the blind man's stick for the poor.
- But for dreams and hopes we will perish.
- Looking forward with expectation and hope will certainly come to fruition.
- Hope is a rocket which takes you farther than you can imagine.
- Hopes keep alive your dreams and dreams your purpose.

HUMAN – BEINGS

- Human beings have the potential to be divine or evil.
- Creation of man is unique in plethora of ways.
- Human life is a rare phenomenon but we have turned it into a drudgery.

- We have no right to call ourselves human beings if we do not attempt to uplift the poor and desolate.
- Every human being is an institution by himself and needs to be admired for that.
- A true human being will never hurt or disparage anybody.

HUMANIST

- It is better to be an atheist and a humanist rather than religious and a misanthrope.

HUMANITY

- Be the aficionado of humanity. If humanity succeeds then it will be a boon to all.
- Your wealth is well spent if spent on improving the lot of humanity.
- Science and religion should be blended to serve humanity.
- All humanity is one single life.
- Be the beacon of humanity and you will become a legend
- True human being is one who shares his riches with others.
- Even a single soul going hungry is a slur on humanity.
- Unstinting support for humanity is true religion.
- Humanity is the most important consideration for any issue.
- Human relationships are the ultimate test of any action.
- We need to harness the potential of all the people to bring peace, progress and prosperity to all.
- True humanity is to have no grouse against anyone and anything.

- Carnage in the name of religion is a slur on humanity.
- You will cruise along when you have no grudge against anyone.
- The greatest endowment of human life is to unleash the potential of all.
- Unstinted commitment to humanity is a virtue worth pursuing.
- Humanity should awaken to the need to provide food, clothing and shelter to all to avoid war and epidemic.
- Every drop of blood we shed is a blow to humanity.
- Unleash your power to redeem the vestiges of humanity.
- We as human beings can either boom or doom depending upon our sincerity towards the prosperity of humanity as a whole.
- Embrace humanity by spreading the message of love and compassion.
- Contempt for the rustic and old is unbecoming of a true human being.
- Every single human being is important however lowly placed he may be.
- When you intend to do harm to another you are harming yourself as you lose your humanity.
- Extending the horizons to cover the entire gamut of humanity is the most worthwhile thing to aspire.
- Champion the cause of humanity and not the parochial interests.
- We human beings should prosper and succeed as a tribe rather than clamouring for individual glories.

- All the hooligans and venal elements should be shown the door if we need a prosperous, peaceful and progressive human society.
- All else is superfluous if at heart you are totally committed to humanity.
- It is a shame on the part of all of us that we are not able to provide food, clothing and shelter to all beings.
- If all people come together and work concertedly then earth will become a paradise.
- The world is for all but the greed of few deprives the majority of their legitimate rights.
- Life becomes simple when you commit yourself to lessen the burden of others.
- All your education and knowledge will be a waste unless you contribute generously to promote the cause of humanity.
- You can elevate your personality to the pinnacle of glory if you are totally committed to humanity.
- Competition kills cooperation thrills.
- Make humanity your passion.
- If humanity has to survive then it has to do away with avarice and selfishness.
- Doing your lot for the underprivileged is far better than chanting the name of god.

HUMBLENESS

- Humble people always achieve glory and greatness.

HUMILITY

- Humility is a virtue that commands great respect.
- Humility is an unparalleled virtue in life.
- Humility has humongous power to mend many things as most people act from ego.
- Humility will enable you to walk into any arena.
- Humility is not the exclusive preserve of the great men.
- Ego manipulates and humility weaves magic.
- In pursuit of knowledge and wisdom maintain total humility lest it may leave you arrogant.
- Fragrance of humility can pervade the whole world.
- With every success you should become more humble as arrogance may spoil your party.
- Set aside your ego while dealing with other people and also while learning from the wise and erudite.
- Humility is an attribute which will open the doors to every place.
- Humility gives respect and gets respect.
- Humility is a degree far better than any of the degrees granted by the best university.
- Humility is divinity.
- Humility is the best gem to adorn a person.
- A wise person is deliberately foolish to manifest his humility.
- Humility adorns knowledge.

- If you are arrogant about your knowledge and wealth then your personality is incomplete as humility is the greatest possession.
- If you are knowledgeable and wealthy you will get tempted to be arrogant but you must make all efforts to be humble.

HUMOUR

- Sense of humour will make you welcome everywhere.
- Be lavish with humour and niggardly with frown.
- Sense of humour in an embarrassing situation is a great virtue.
- Human life bereft of humour is worthless.

HUNGER

- A morsel of food is far more valuable than money for the hungry.
- Hunger for praise is worse than hunger for food.
- A morsel of food will be relished when poignantly hungry.
- Foraging when hungry is foolishness rather provision them in advance.
- Profanity is acceptable but not dereliction of hungry human beings.
- Only one who has been hungry can relish the food.

HYPOCRISY

- We hate people who lie, however we excuse ourselves for committing the same sin.

- We expect others to forgive our mistakes but we find it difficult to forgive others.
- Societal pressure is the reason we behave unlike ourselves.
- A debonair will never show contempt for other people.
- A narcissist is better than a hypocrite.
- Societal pressure makes us present our personality in variance to our true self.
- It is hypocrisy to build monuments for those whose ideals we do not emulate.

IDEAS

- Always be open to new ideas as dogmatism leads to moribund.
- Keep trying new ideas and concepts and that would keep you young.
- Profusion of ideas should be encouraged to capitalize on them.
- Profusion of ideas need to be encouraged and seized to make the most of them.
- An idea has the potential to make you prosperous if acted upon spontaneously without waiting for opportune time.
- When you are possessed with an idea then you are just unstoppable.
- Keep replenishing your mind with new ideas.

IDOLS

- Adoration of your idols should not render you a persona non-grata.

IGNORANCE

- Ignorance breeds arrogance.
- Arrogance emanates from ignorance. An ignorant mind is like a dungeon causing claustrophobia.

IMAGINATION

- Stretch your imagination to the ultimate frontiers and work on it passionately and you will relish every moment of it.
- Great imagination has the potential to receive abundance if it is put into action.
- Imagination can colour your life.
- Push your imagination farthest and expect that to come true and it certainly will.
- Unfurl your power of imagination and try to put substance into that.

IMPACT

- Your reward is proportionate to how many lives you impact through your service.

IMPATIENCE

- Most of the tragedies in life is the result of impatience and arrogance.
- Trivial matters snowball into crisis if impatiently handled.
- Arrogance and impatience have spoiled many a relationships.
- Impatience leads to anger and anger leads to disaster.

- Impatience often leads to anger and anger to anguish.
- We are always impatient to know the result and we precipitate the matter.
- More often than not impatience is the reason for tussle.
- Impatience leads to anger and anger leads to disaster.

INERTIA

- State of inertia is the greatest force to counter.

INFLEXIBILITY

- More often that not we do not allow leeway to others to transform themselves.

INITIATIVE

- Do not forfeit your initiative – you will always languish.
- Never stop taking initiatives to better your life and that of others.
- Challenge yourself to take initiative on your plans.
- Be in the forefront to do good and a bystander in doing bad.
- Our initiatives will decide our future.
- We are so much overawed by the great leaders that we do not take initiative to do something for the society.
- The music in you will die down if you fail to take initiatives in the direction of your dreams.
- Lack of skill and talent is no excuse to not embark upon something worthwhile and purposeful.

INNOVATION

- Innovation and creativity takes you out of the drudgery of daily routine.
- Keep innovating to beat the mundane routine.
- Constant innovation provides a lot of enthusiasm and rewards.

INTROSPECTION

- Beauty of introspection is beyond words.
- Introspection is the best tool in your repertoire.
- Look unto yourself to understand life.
- Use introspection as a tool to self-discovery.
- Look within yourself and you will be surprised to find a person with unlimited potential.
- Probe within you the fragile and negative qualities, do away with them and achieve greatness.

INVESTMENT

- Spending time in reading good books is the best investment of time.

INVOLVEMENT

- Involve in every good thing to evolve as a human being.
- Look at things oblivious of the fact that you are involved in them.
- The moment you lose yourself in things you hardly have time to fret.

JEALOUSY

- Jealousy ruins us and does no harm to whom it is directed.
- Green-eyed monster called jealousy will only make you a living funeral of your self.
- Jealousy is a fire we are igniting on the stack of hay in us.
- Jealousy makes you crazier than the person creating jealousy.

JOURNEY

- Journey is more momentous than the destination.
- Don't gloat over your accomplishments as your journey has just begun.
- Enjoying the journey is as important as the destination.
- Enjoy the journey as not doing so will leave you flustered at the destination.
- It is the journey to your coveted goal which is more pleasurable than the reaching of goals.

JOY

- Work is worship only if you enjoy doing that.
- Treat every situation as a joyous one and you will be surprised everything is filled with joy.
- Singing songs of joy while you are working is a sign of your happiness.
- Even the smallest things can give you so much of joy that the big things may not.

- Find joy in everything you do and you will never be stressed up.

KINDNESS

- Kind words soothe the hurt soul.

KNOWLEDGE

- Quench the thirst for knowledge and that would reward you abundantly.
- Action without knowledge is destined to fail.
- Knowledge is more powerful than the universe itself.
- Replenish your knowledge to avoid moribund.
- Pursuit of knowledge to enrich oneself is chicanery.
- Spending money in the pursuit of knowledge is better than on luxuries.
- Investment in knowledge will reap rich rewards.
- Exams are the test of memory rather than that of knowledge.
- No amount of money is enough to pursue knowledge.
- Pursuit of knowledge may provide you wealth but pursuit of wealth may not provide knowledge.
- In the twenty first century knowledge has become the lingua franca of all.
- Light of knowledge dispels the darkness of ignorance.
- Quench the thirst for knowledge rather than that of wealth.
- Dissemination of knowledge at affordable cost will bring peace, progress and prosperity to the entire human race.

- Gather all the knowledge you can but commit yourself to using it to the advantage of all.
- Seek knowledge and you will get wealth and seek wealth and you lose everything if you resort to unethical means.
- Pretend to be a fool to gain knowledge from others.
- Unless knowledge acquired is used for the benefit of all it is of no use.
- We need to accept the new paradigm of knowledge–based economy.
- Power of confidence sans knowledge may lead to a fiasco.
- Dissemination of knowledge is vital to uplift people from ignorance and poverty.
- The whole universe is there to enhance knowledge; merely procuring degrees does not make you wise.
- Acquiring knowledge should be a life long process and also using that for the benefit of all.
- Quest for knowledge is a very valuable thing.
- Knowledge is wealth which multiplies when you spend and share.
- Thirst for knowledge is more amazing than thirst for material things.
- Knowledge with poverty is better than wealth without knowledge.
- Dissemination of knowledge abundantly at a low cost will ensure a salubrious society.

LAUGHTER

- Laughter is one of the greatest gifts human beings have.
- Laughter is the antidote for any problem.
- If you can laugh at your own gaffes then you will always have loads of fun.
- Laughter is a tonic for good health.

LEADER

- Treating everyone with respect is the mark of a great leader.
- All the harangue and demagogue by the pseudo leaders are to take the gullible masses for a ride.
- Leaders need to set an exemplary example for the followers to emulate.
- Pseudo leaders promise heaven and deliver hell.
- For a true leader, position and authority are of no consequence.
- True leaders need no ministerial positions to do social good.
- A manager always catches people under him doing wrong things whereas a leader catches people doing the right things.
- Leadership involves the heart and manager ship involves the mind but ultimately it is the heart that wins.

LEADERSHIP

- Leadership entails trust and selflessness.
- Leadership need not ensue from authority as anybody with a service-oriented approach can get it.

LEARNING

- If you stop learning, you stop growing.
- Every moment spent in learning is very beneficial.
- Exams take away the fun out of learning.
- Learning from every experience without bitterness makes you wiser.
- Always look for ways to learn from every situation and person.
- Children should be encouraged to evolve their own method of learning.
- Earning is hidden inside learning.
- Learning should be a perennial experience as there is no limit to learning.
- Look for avenues to learn and earn.
- Learning new skills will keep you young.
- Learning new things will keep old age away.
- Learn from the erudite and scholarly the philosophy of life and perseverance from the successful men.
- Never be complacent with the knowledge and wisdom you have as there is lot to explore and understand.
- Life is not a struggle but a pleasant learning opportunity.
- There is so much to learn in the world that it is futile to dwell on negatives.
- Turn every bitter experience into a better lesson which will guide you in future.

- Never cease pursuing knowledge and wisdom as that will keep you ever fresh.
- Broaden your horizons by learning new languages, ideas and culture of other people.
- The more you learn, the more you realize that the journey is pretty long.
- Learning from one's own experience will take a life time. Rather learning from other's experience is wise.

LENDING

- Lend not more than what you can afford to lose.

LESSON

- Problems teach you valuable lessons.
- Seek wisdom from the old and dynamism from the youth.
- No effort is wasted if you learn the lesson.
- Nothing goes waste in life if we learn worthy things from the experiences.
- Never be scared of trying something new and failing as you will certainly gain something in the form of learning valuable lessons.
- Every event has a lesson hidden in it for you to turn it into wisdom.
- Every one is capable of teaching worthwhile lessons. So don't underestimate anybody.

LIFE

- In spite of all its attendant problems, life is full of miracles.
- Celebrate the festivals and anniversaries of all as if your own and you will relish life like never before.
- Do not drown yourself in the deluge of mundane things. It may stop you from enjoying life's small pleasures.
- Life without upheavals is insipid.
- Simplify your life as that would vastly enhance your power and save vital resources.
- Being a parent is not merely giving life but to give living.
- Treat your life partner as a friend and a part of you to enjoy bliss.
- Write your own obituary and live in the reverse.
- Primordial life was much simpler and joyful.
- When you are close to death do you realize the value of life?
- The more deep you get into the mysteries of life the more esoteric it becomes.
- Celebrate life every moment.
- Relish every moment as it will vanish in a twinkle.
- Happiness and sadness are like the waxing and waning of moon.
- Life is a rare gift, do not squander it on rift.
- Life can be magical or tragical depending on your choice.
- Shape your life in the way you yearn in spite of obstacles.
- Live life as if death is lurking around the corner.
- Let others emulate your life rather than doling out advices.

- Life is like ocean tides with its low and the highs.
- Human life is a great miracle and should not be squandered on frivolous things.
- You are as old as the primordial and as fresh as the dew.
- Life is too short to be spent on enmity.
- When death is lurking around the corner man realizes the importance of life.
- A scrupulous life is a sign of maturity.
- Life is a marathon where we need to have proper balance of stamina and pace.
- Don't meander through life mechanically.
- Your life is not enough to learn from your own mistakes.
- Human life is so rare that not even a moment should be wasted on trivial things.
- It's a tragedy how people spend their life on mundane things.
- Live every moment of life fully as time is irretrievable.
- Engaging in squabbles is a colossal waste of time as you are squandering precious moments of your life.
- Every moment spent on envy, gossip, complaint and anger is every moment of precious life lost for ever.
- We are so caught in the quagmire of mundane things we stop wondering about the gifts of life.
- Taking things for granted takes the fun and joy from life.
- Life is a humongous conundrum which is difficult to understand.
- Enthusiasm, excitement and eagerness blended together have the potential to enliven your life.

- Anger, fear, worry, doubt and negative things sap your energy and make your life needlessly miserable.
- Meandering through life wantonly is a colossal waste of a precious gift.
- Life is a rarest of the rare gift which we should cherish and relish.
- If you keep marvelling and exploring the beauty of nature you will be filled with zest.
- Live life every moment as if that is the last as you never know your end.
- Life is a temptations galore ensnaring you to fall into the pitfall.
- Life is not about time but quality experiences.
- Beautiful diamond has to undergo a lot of processing so is the diamond of life.
- Don't be a bystander in the game of life.
- Living life for principles requires greater determination and abstinence from temptations.
- If life is not for fun then it certainly is not for gun.
- Treat real life as reel life and reel life as real life to fully exploit life.
- Life is a roulette dishing out crisis and opportunities turn by turn.
- Life is a carte blanche to be en cashed by us by deciding the dream with a deadline.
- Pursuit of goals should not become such an obsession that you forget to live.

- Millions of people scrape through life eking out a life without understanding the purpose of life.
- By indulging in vices, skirmishes, anger, negativity, criticism, complaining and cynicism we are squandering the best gift of nature; life.
- If you want to live fully then set aside all negative things.
- Life is meant to be lived on your own terms as living on others' will make you a caricature of them.
- If you are all the time improving, enthusiastic, learning, loving and serving you certainly are living life to the full.
- Beauty of life is when we don't take anything seriously but enjoy every moment of it.
- Life is mired with both bouquets and brickbats.Take it in the proper perspective to cherish both.
- We are so much involved in mundane things that we cease to live a life.
- Waiting to live life sometime in future is squandering the most precious gift.
- Time is of little essence if you are living life fully.
- Accept life as a wonderful miracle and expect miracles.
- Living a vegetable existence is the horrendous use of the most wonderful gift of nature.
- Imagine the wonders you want in your life and start reverse planning to get them.
- Play act in life as if you are acting in a movie where you are not emotionally connected with the character.
- The very fact that you are alive is itself a great miracle.
- Its life and not time that is the essence.

- Fill every moment with enthusiasm, verve and zest to make life wonderful.
- Life becomes insipid when you reach the state of ennui.
- Bemoaning everything is a sign of cynicism and regretting the great gift of life.
- Living life for the world at large will reap rich benefits and you will always keep exuding happiness.
- Always turn every moment into a momentous one as that is what is life all about.
- Human life has no meaning if it is not used to elevate the world into a better place to live.
- A worthwhile life is one which has everyone in the ambit of its life.
- Crescendo of life is so magical that you can dance to your satisfaction.
- Take life each moment as it is a miracle.
- Life is tough for the lazy and a miracle for the assiduous person.
- Keep smiling, enjoy every moment and have fun in life.
- Live life for others and your life will be golden.
- Human life is precious but we treat it with contempt.
- Life is tough but still worth it.
- Human life is the greatest gift and miracle.
- Live every moment of your life lest they go into the oblivion.
- Human life is a rare gift which should not be squandered on trivial things.

- Make your life simple and focus on only your coveted goal.
- You will never get a chance to live the same moments again. So make the most of them.
- Repent not your age as many are not fortunate enough to live as long as you.
- Our life is so serendipitous that we cannot imagine how everything came into being.
- Human beings have got so much mired in routine things that they are abusing the greatest gift called life.
- You are as limitless as the limitless universe.
- Life should be such that every moment you rejoice and enjoy and not fret.
- Life throws challenges at you to fortify your personality.
- Living life to your heart's content is possible only if you help others do the same.
- Always being serious takes away the charm from life.
- Spending your energy in positive direction and good purpose is vital for a great life.
- There is no greater miracle and magic than life itself.
- Life is evolving every moment.
- Do not allow the dew drops of every moment to go waste.
- Life comes but once so realize your full potential.
- Lives becomes insipid because we do not venture into new things or old things with new perceptions.

- Life's struggles are evolutionary in nature as they make you strong if you take it in the proper perspective.
- Life will be tragic if you do not treat life as a magic.
- The very fact that you have meandered through life's maze is miraculous and you are cut out for great things.
- Meandering through life moaning and groaning fritters away the very essence of life.

LIGHT

- Look in the direction of light and you can avoid shadows.

LISTEN

- Listening with rapt attention is real communication. Listen to the experienced and the wise to enhance your personality.

LIVING

- A proper blend of materialism and spiritualism is essential for a good living. Proper balance in everything is vital to good living.
- Live up to your own expectations.
- There is a vast difference between living and mere existence.
- It is more daunting to be a part of society and still be peaceful than becoming a hermit staying far away from the maddening crowd.
- Have a penchant for living life with zest, fervor and love.

LOVE

- Shower love and happiness on every creature – you will receive an avalanche of happiness.
- Love is a lingua franca of the world.
- Love is a panacea for most ills.
- Love is a miracle potion which can cure every disease.
- Love can cure all malaise.
- Love is an ambrosia and hatred venom.
- Universal love is essential to make you a true human being.
- Drink the potion of love and become immortal.
- Sublime love is the magic potion for all ills.
- All the doors are open for a man possessing love for whole of humanity.
- Love should be the motivation and not fear, as it is more sweet and enduring.
- If you say something out of love that must get reflected in your tone and demeanor.
- Sublime love is all pervasive.
- Loving all humanity will make you the cynosure of all eyes.
- Unconditional love is easy to preach and difficult to practice.
- A loving heart will have no malice towards anyone.
- True love is sublime and universal in nature.
- Gather all the honey of love without getting stung by bees of criticism.
- Religion of love is paramount and leaves no room for hatred.

- Mesmerize people by your charisma of love and character.
- When you are bitten by the bug of love you are just unstoppable.
- Make others your slaves through your love and grace.
- Love can transform enmity into friendship.
- Love emanating from craving for carnal pleasures is demeaning and not sublime.
- Fall in subtle love with life and bliss will ensue.
- In the presence of love all the barriers break.
- Love is sublime, divine and immortal.
- True love never wants to possess.
- Love is the greatest armor with no chinks.
- If love is the motivator, everything will turn out to be great.
- True love is love for all the things in the universe.
- Love is the elixir of extraordinary life.
- Gather honey by sprinkling love on your way.
- Love has the potential to transform human society into a garden of Eden.
- Love is a divine gift which grows with every use.
- Character, humility and love for all human beings and whole of universe are your best friends.
- Love is more powerful than logic.
- Things bought out of love lasts longer than that bought out of obligation.
- Absence of love makes relationships sour and irreconcilable.
- Paradise is within you and not elsewhere if you have abundant love for the whole universe.

MALICE

- Malice towards anybody is inimical to oneself.
- Have no malice towards anyone as you will be carrying the burden in your mind.
- To berate others in public gaze is superciliousness and is a disrespect to humanity.

MANAGER

- Managers should not indulge in cavil but be the facilitator to get the best out of their subordinates.

MARRIAGE

- Marriage is a unique institution which deserves all the adorations and accolades.
- Marriage is a life long commitment to share happiness and adversities together.
- Marriage is an impeccable relationship which requires constant nurturing and understanding.
- Marriage is an institution requiring commitment from both the partners.
- Marriage is an institution so sacred that it involves shared vision, misfortunes, happiness, love, friendship and et al and not solely physical relationships.

MATERIALISM

- Too much reliance on material things for happiness is a chimera.

- Material things possess you and not the other way round.
- Happiness from material things is evanescent.
- Materialism is a scourge we are all suffering without thought to the welfare of others.
- Materialistic ambitions throw caution to winds and also makes you resort to unethical means.
- Materialism is a quicksand where you can get stuck.

MATURITY

- Do not get into skirmishes as they are the signs of immaturity.
- Arrogance is the sign of immaturity and humility a sign of maturity.

MAVERICK

- Be a maverick as you will achieve something sensational and serendipity will smile on you.
- A maverick will have no fear of criticism and adverse situations.
- Break every rule if they do not support the dictates of your conscience.
- Challenge the tradition and blaze the trail by travelling the untreaded path.
- Swimming against the current requires you to be a maverick and a trail blazer.
- Stray away from the beaten track and you will have blazed the trail.

MIND

- An idle mind is a breeding ground for evils.
- There are many monsters in your mind those need to be eliminated.
- Brain works wonders when it is free from worries.
- Your mind is a fertile land where weeds and good plants can grow The choice is entirely in your hands.
- One can withstand physical agony but mental agony is difficult to bear.
- Mental agony is much worse than physical pain.
- Your mind must work like a fountain to sustain the proliferation of ideas.
- Human mind readily accepts negative things and avoids positive things.
- Tongue works faster than mind when there is clutter in the mind.
- Flurry of thoughts emanate from your mind and overwhelm you if you do not control them.
- Mind is the villain or hero depending on the way it thinks and executes the thoughts.
- Your stature is reduced to zero when you stand before a mighty ocean but your mind is more deeper than the last ocean.
- Mental toughness begets physical toughness.
- Physical affliction and malignancy is far better than a confused mind.
- Keep removing the cobwebs from your mind and you will add quality to your life.
- Cleanse your mind of filth and weeds lest your mind becomes

a barren land with unwanted vegetation.

- Your mind is also an agricultural land. You can plant any tree you want.
- Having an unbiased mind is a great virtue.
- Keep a record of all your ideas and thoughts as your mind cannot remember them.
- Your mind is a fountain head of thoughts which can elevate you to the acme.
- A sword may kill a person but not make his mind a slave.
- Body is a donkey and mind is a horse not meaning to belittle the hard-working donkey.
- Human body has limitations but the mind has none.
- There are more reptiles you need to root out from your mind than outside.

MIRACLE

- Every sun rise is the harbinger of many miracles.
- It is better to work believing in miracles than blindly waiting for miracles to occur by itself.
- If you are not happy about the miracle of life you are the most unfortunate being.
- Miracles happen when we believe in them.
- Plethora of miracles have made us feel ennui rather than gratitude.
- Miracles abound where there is faith, hope and enthusiasm.
- The greatest miracle of universe is that everything evolved from nothing.

- Universe will unravel its wonders to the one who is altruistic, wise and compassionate.
- Every moment is a miracle but our ego thinks otherwise.
- Human life itself is the greatest miracle which we squander on useless pursuits.
- Failing to realize that human life itself is the greatest miracle is the cause for all sadness.
- Miracles emanate from commitment, action and perseverance.
- Being skeptical about miracle is an aberration as everything in the universe is nothing short of miracle.
- If you keep counting the miracles of life and universe you will never waste your time on criticizing, complaining and condemning.
- Don't count your age in years rather count in moments of joy.
- Every moment is more than a piece of diamond.
- Every moment is a gift to the enlightened and boredom to the ignoramus.
- Cheer every moment lest you lose on life.
- A moment may change your life for ever.
- Make every moment momentous.
- Enjoy every moment of your life as the sands of life are slipping by.
- You can change your life at a moment's notice.
- Rejoice every moment as that may be your last.
- Reminisce the nostalgic moments of the past and dump the nightmares.
- Every moment is precious to garnish your personality.

- Rewards and recognition may provide you with lot of excitement and euphoria but they are ephemeral.
- Relishing every moment is a far better option than ruing every moment.
- Seize fleeting moments of joy lest you repent.
- You can relish every moment if you watch the world with wonder and excitement.
- Treasure moments of glory and bury moments of misery to feel elated.
- Treat every moment with respect as it may render miracles you never imagined or expected.
- Every moment must be used to enrich your personality.
- Live life in the moment and do not worry about future and ruminating about past.
- Every moment is precious and should not be wasted in negative thinking.
- Every moment is too precious that it should be used to better yourself.
- Every moment is too precious to be squandered on futile things.
- Make magical moments of your life momentous.
- It takes only a moment to change your life depending on your intention and commitment.
- Every moment is pregnant with miracles.
- Every moment can either be a speck of diamond or a particle of dust. It depends on how you use.
- Each moment is a different reality.
- Every moment you spend time, energy and money in acquiring knowledge and wisdom is well spent.

- Moments of joy should be treasured and that of despair be buried.

MIRAGE

- Name, fame and fortune are just a mirage.

MISFORTUNE

- The lesson learnt from misfortune is better than that of fortune.
- Callous attitude towards the misfortunes of others is a sign of immaturity.

MOMENT

- Don't count your age in years rather count in moments of joy.
- Every moment is more than a piece of diamond.
- Every moment is a gift to the enlightened.
- Cheer every moment lest you lose on life.
- A moment may change your life for ever.
- Make every moment momentous.
- Enjoy every moment of your life as the sands of life are slipping by.
- You can change your life at a moment's notice.
- Rejoice every moment as that may be your last.
- Every moment is precious to garnish your personality.

- Rewards and recognition may provide you with lot of excitement and euphoria but they are ephemeral.
- Relishing every moment is a far better option than ruing every moment.
- Seize fleeting moments of joy lest you repent.
- You can relish every moment if you watch the world with wonder and excitement.
- Treasure moments of glory and bury moments of misery to feel elated.
- Treat every moment with respect as it may render miracles you never imagined or expected.
- Every moment must be used to enrich your personality.
- Live life in the moment and do not worry about future and ruminating about past.
- Every moment is precious and should not be wasted in negative thinking.
- Every moment is too precious that it should be used to better yourself.
- Every moment is too precious to be squandered on futile things.
- Make magical moments of your life momentous.
- It takes only a moment to change your life depending on your intention and commitment.
- Every moment is pregnant with miracles.
- Every moment can either be a speck of diamond or a particle of dust. It depends on how you use.
- Each moment is a different reality.

- Every moment you spend time, energy and money in acquiring knowledge and wisdom is well spent.
- Moments of joy should be treasured and that of despair be buried.

MOMENTUM

- Exert pressure on inertia and that will provide momentum.
- Keep moving as halting is stagnation and will result in cesspool.
- Fantasizing about future is a worthwhile exercise as it provides momentum to your purpose.
- Inertia of the mind is responsible for laziness.
- Once you give momentum to your thinking and implement it immediately, it will reward you richly.

MONEY

- Money can play magic or havoc depending on who holds it.
- Pursuit of education for making money is mercenary.
- Money is a boon or curse depending upon the holder.
- Niggardliness in spending money is tantamount to beggary.
- Money is the root of all evils because it has gotten into the wrong hands.
- Make money work for you and not otherwise as you tend to become slave to it.
- Money should not be the guiding factor in building a relationship.
- Making money is not by itself bad but how and for what is

the moot question.

- Money is a knife which can kill or cure depending on whose hands it is.
- Too little and too much of money both are dangerous.
- Flies swarm around honey and greedy around money.

MORALE

- Boost your sagging morale by enthusiasm and even fake confidence.

MORALITY

- Morality is the backbone of society.
- Immoral things thrive when we have no consideration for others.
- An illiterate without morality is less dangerous than a literate without morality.
- Amorality is the order of the day but the pristine glory of morality will continue to sustain.

MOTIVATION

- Managing others is not to maneuver them but to motivate them.
- Happiness ensues as a choice and does not depend on external things.
- A scorned person may cause harm to himself and others.
- Success eludes us when we are short on enthusiasm and perseverance.

- Egalitarian society is a pipe dream as it kills the motivation.
- A word of encouragement is all that is required to provide motivation to many.

MUSIC

- Mellifluous music is better than a pill for your malady.
- Mellifluousness of music can do wonders to the psyche.
- You find so much of solace in music that you are transported to another world.
- Music is mellifluous to the ears.

NATURE

- Nature itself is a great source of knowledge.
- Denuding the forests is akin to denuding ourselves.
- Nature needs to be nurtured to have a sustainable world.
- Reverence for nature and the universe is a must for all.
- Marauding nature in the name of development is ungratefulness of the worst kind.
- Don't awaken the sleeping giant called nature to wreak havoc.
- Human insanity looks preposterous when looked from the perspective of evolution which has taken millions of years.
- Nurture nature to beautify our lives.
- Let us put an end to the scramble and plundering of nature.
- We need to respect the nature which is a succor to all.
- Treat your body with respect as it is a priceless gift of nature.

- No words are enough to admire and be grateful to nature for the gift of life.
- We are so embroiled in daily chores that we stop wondering at the beauty of the nature and miracles of life.
- Pitfalls are the ways of nature to test your potential and tenacity.
- We need to retrieve the glory of nature as it was in the pristine times.
- If you are kind to nature there will be magic and if you are cruel to nature there will be havoc.
- Catastrophe is looming large if we continue to play havoc with ecology and environment.
- Keep savoring the wonders of the nature that you will have no time to worry.
- Nature will seek retribution for all the onslaughts made on it unless human beings respect nature and restore the pristine glory of nature.
- Brief time that nature has endowed us should be utilized to ameliorate the condition of humanity.
- Human beings always crib about weather conditions even though it is nature's way of sustaining flora and fauna.
- Ravishing the nature will lead to calamity.
- Nature has given everything free but we charge for everything.
- Man thinks he is great but is nothing compared to the marvels of nature.
- Keep wondering at nature and you will never have a boring moment.

- Hand over your affairs to nature and you will enjoy every moment.
- Nature is full of ambrosia if you think profoundly.
- We should be thankful to nature for sustaining us and giving us life.
- Be an ally to the nature and you will enjoy total bliss.
- Bounty of nature is available to all if they have a purpose in life.
- We are obliged to nature to make it more beautiful and wonderful.
- Nature is a perennial source of inspiration.
- Never complain about weather as that is a gift from nature which created everything.
- Going against nature invites catastrophe.
- Nature you ravish, it will have you famish.
- Nature's miracles are incredible compared to the inventions of mankind.
- If we respect nature as divinity we need not get into the debate of whether God exists or not.
- Nature is so bountiful in its gifts to us that even a life time is not enough to be grateful for it.

NEGATIVITY

- Insulate yourself against negative people and thoughts.
- Ruminating over negative thoughts puts you in a quandary.
- Beware of the soothsayer, naysayer and complainers.
- Never indulge in negativity as it takes away the joy from life.

- Complaining, condemning and criticizing will only complicate the matter.
- Don't squander your energy in argument, envy, hatred and jealousy rather use it to your benefit of becoming worthier.
- Remove all the venom of negativity from your being as it may lead to cynicism.
- Negativity clogs your mind and blocks your progress.
- You may prove to be your own nemesis if you house cynicism, negativity, self-doubt and fear.
- Always living in the shadow of fear and worry leaves you paralyzed .
- Rid yourself of all negative feelings of anger, hatred, jealousy, pessimism and worry to free your mind to think clearly.
- Even a moment lost in negativity is irretrievable that you will repent later.
- There will never be respite from negativity unless you replace them with positive thoughts.
- Never have hatred, jealousy and criticism as part of your life.
- Don't get involved in gossip, skirmishes and criticism as that would sap your energy and take you far away from your goal.
- Never criticize, complain and condemn as that would make you feel bad and precipitate the matter.
- Worry and tension paralyses our rational mind and leaves us groping in the dark.
- Anger, hatred, jealousy, pessimism are insidious matters.
- It is common to believe negative news and doubt the positive news.

- Never provide asylum to negative thoughts as it may leave you shattered.

NOSTALGIA

- You can never turn back the clock but can relish the nostalgic memories of the past.
- Nostalgia makes you reminisce the past glory.

OPPORTUNITY

- Opportunities come masquerading as problems.
- You have plethora of opportunities if you are free from preconceived notions.
- Value of an opportunity is realized after it passes away unencashed.
- Seize every opportunity to do good to others as that will ensure your own happiness.
- Treat problems and crisis as an opportunity to grow spiritually.
- Welcome each day as an opportunity to improve your personality.
- Don't complain about the dearth of opportunities as there are many which go unnoticed.
- Never ever complain about lack of opportunities as there are plenty of them if you observe properly.
- Treat every day as an opportunity to be the harbinger of good things.
- Make hay when the anger is away.

- Opportunities favour people with positive attitude and enthusiasm.
- All the doors will open to new vista for a man of passion, purpose and humility.
- Every single moment is an opportunity to realize your coveted dream.
- Every challenge is an opportunity for you to manifest your mettle.
- Train your eyes on opportunities and not crisis.
- There is no dearth of opportunities for the one with an open mind and is not rigid.
- Opportunities arise every moment if you are aware of them and make use of it to your advantage.
- Surfeit of opportunities open up for a person who has courage and confidence.
- You will always find opportunities to be of help to others and that will win you respect.
- There are plethora of talents in you but little opportunity to capitalize on them because you lack self-belief, confidence.
- Opportunity comes to those who are willing to take risks.
- Opportunities are abundant for a man with enthusiasm and alertness.
- Make the most of opportunities as they may not come again irrespective of whether you succeed or fail.
- Never spare an opportunity to harness your potential and personality.

OPTIMISM

- Life is full of miracles for the optimist.
- Over optimism is far better than a die hard pessimism.
- It is better to be a die-hard optimist than a rueful pessimist.
- Don't be overawed by volatility of the situation as your optimism will tackle everything.
- There is surfeit of opportunities for those with positive mind and alertness.
- A die-hard optimism is better than an outright cynicism.
- Make a funeral of all the negatives and burn the candle of positivity to proceed towards your goal.
- Having a positive outlook takes care of umpteen number of hurdles.

ORATORY

- Oratory skills should not be used for rabble rousing.

ORIGINAL

- Being your original self is better than being a caricature of someone.
- Following in other's footsteps should be avoided and you must set your own agenda.

PANIC

- Never panic even in the gravest situation as that may result in disaster.
- Undue panic paralyses your rational thinking and puts you and others into jeopardy.

PASSION

- Passion with vision takes you to your mission.
- Passion is a horse on which you can stride to your goal.
- Doing your work with passion will assure you your mission.
- Stoke the simmering passions in you to attain your mission.
- Treat work as a passion and you will never rue it.
- Incinerate your passions to reach your mission.
- You will discover that you have unlimited energy for things you love the most. Then why waste on things you don't love?
- You can unleash your energies on things you love the most and put on reins your energy on which you don't.
- Keep stoking the simmering passions in you to reach your ultimate goal and purpose.
- Passion sans vision will lead you nowhere.
- Passion coupled with purpose will take you to great heights.

PAST

- Your past follows you like your own shadow tormenting you perpetually.
- Never let the ghosts of your past to scare away the present.
- Looking behind at the past may result in accident in present jeopardizing your future.
- Unless we forget the nightmares of the past the present becomes a nightmare.

- Don't rake up the past as it stinks and leaves a bad taste and spoils relationships.
- If you look behind you are sure to meet with an accident as you are not focusing on what is ahead in life.
- Many people are so much obsessed with the past that they are always driving in the reverse gear.

PATIENCE

- Patience can achieve more than valor.
- Power of patience is more formidable than a rock.
- In a marathon of life patience is the vital virtue.
- Patience is the key to growth.
- Patience is a virtue worth developing to reach the acme of greatness.
- It is better to have patience than series of impatience which results in agony.
- A modicum of patience can go a long way in getting things through.
- Unbridled patience makes things simple.
- Put off your anger for a while and the situation becomes friendly.
- To maintain sanity in this chaotic world requires unparalleled patience.
- Patience is an endurance test to make you wiser.
- Stretch your patience further when anger is about to burst and the results will be astounding.
- Withstand all the trials and tribulations while pursuing your purpose in life.

- Patience is a great virtue.
- Success comes to those who have patience.
- Patience for some moments before acting can stall many tragedies and crises.

PEACE

- A tranquil mind conquers all.
- Most difficult thing is to have peace with oneself.
- Direct all your efforts in peacefully changing the world for better.
- Peace without progress is better than progress without peace.
- Calm and quiet wins the peace.
- A brokered peace is better than a holy war.

PERCEPTION

- Simple things are complex and complex things are simple depending on your perception.
- Change your perception and your life is transformed.
- Life is full of mirth and joy provided you perceive it to be so.
- Life is either a comedy or tragedy depending on your perception.
- Crooked perceptions will make you feel everything is crooked.
- Your perceptions about the world makes the world like that.
- Change your perception and you change the world.

- If you look at the world and nature with wonder and excitement your life will be filled with happiness.
- It is all about perception for all the aspects of life.
- It is your perception that interprets problems as opportunities or a pitfall.
- Always imagining bad things is not good for you as precious time is wasted on that.
- Our perception decides our outlook in life.
- Parochial and paranoid attitude is the reason for our biased perceptions.
- Gregariousness is both a strength and weakness depending on your perceptions.
- Grief and happiness are just a matter of perception.
- Heaven and hell are a matter of perception.
- Treat the world as paradise and you will see everything beautiful and treat the world as hell and you see misery everywhere.
- Eyes see what the mind dictates.
- The world looks in a hue depending upon the colour of our glasses we wear.
- Your ability to do things depends upon your perception about yourself.

PERSEVERANCE

- In spite of failures keep going towards your coveted goal and you will be surprised by the results.

PERSONALITY

- Polish yourself every moment to garnish your personality.
- Spend your time in garnishing your personality.
- Be like a coconut, tough from outside and soft inside.
- Garnish your personality with grace and humility.
- Your conscience should be as tough as the diamond and your heart as soft as rose petals.
- Garnish your personality with character, principles, ethics and wisdom.
- Our personalities are like an onion which has labyrinth of layers revealing more as you peel.
- Bringing out the best in dire circumstances proves your character, tenacity and perseverance.
- The more you polish the stone of your personality more it will turn out to be a diamond.

PHILOSOPHY

- A philosophy in life is like oxygen to the body.
- Philosophy is the perennial source of happiness.

PLUNDER

- Plundering natural wealth is inimical to the interests of humanity.
- Plundering nature is cataclysmic rather we should evolve sustainable growth as that will be beneficial to all.

POSSESSION

- When you lament for not possessing something, visualize the plight of persons living in subhuman conditions.
- Becoming restless when you lose something is akin to being possessed by things.
- We want to possess things which we may not need but just to flaunt your wares.
- When possessions posses you then its time you dispossess them.

POTENTIAL

- Human beings are endowed with immense potentiality.
- Money is a potent force that can be used for constructive or destructive use.
- Ignorance of one's potential is the greatest hurdle to self-discovery.
- Harness your potential on a continual basis to achieve your coveted goal.
- We need to unravel the latent potential in every person to create a salubrious society.
- Unless you challenge yourself to do the impossible you will never test your potential.
- Look upon your own potential as colossal to achieve something worthwhile.
- Human beings have the capacity to do wonders but it is a tragedy that they spend their time and energy in decimating others.
- There is so much of potential within us even if we are not educated if only we foray into unknown frontiers.

- You have phenomenal potential if you care to foray into what you conceive and believe.
- When you believe in your own potential you need no certificate from the world.
- Our mind has the potential to visualize and execute all our dreams if we put that into action.
- Keep probing and challenging your mind's capacity and you will be astounded by its potential.
- There is mind-boggling potential in each of us if only we fathom our brains.
- Internet has humongous potential to impart knowledge if you have time to spare and proper choice.
- Everyone has tremendous potential if only we encourage them to take risks.
- Human potential is like an onion .It has many layers as you keep peeling, more is revealed about yourself.

PRACTICE

- An ounce of practice is better than tons of theory.

PRAISE

- Keep praising those with low self-esteem and they will be grateful to you. Adoration of others is good but self-praise is also vital.
- Lavish praise can do wonders and criticism will undo all the good.
- Spontaneous praise is much better than a belated generosity.

- Be generous with praise and niggardly with criticism.
- Be niggardly with words unless used for praise.
- Praise can do wonders whereas criticism can play havoc.
- Never clamor for praise and recognition as you will be open to exploitation.
- Never ever be thirsty of praise and accolades when you do something good as that may lead to frustration.
- You have every right to admire yourself for all the good you have done.
- Be a praise-giver and not a fault-finder as praising boosts the confidence and fault-finding undermines.
- Praise yourself when you do a Samaritan job as that will boost your morale to do more.
- Always praise others with alacrity and you will enjoy others' respect.
- Keep waxing the good in everybody and the bad will wane automatically.

PRECEPTS

- All precepts are futile without implementation.

PRESENT

- Past is a ghost present is a toast and future a host.
- Regretting the past and brooding about future makes the magical moment of the present futile.
- We carry the burden of the past and the anxiety about future to render the precious present miserable.

- Every moment has the potential to transform your life if you live in the present.
- Remove the shackles of the past and anxieties of future to live cheerfully in the present.
- The precious moments of your life should not be spent about repenting the past and being anxious about the future, rather focus on the present which will make your present and future extremely good.
- Putting off living life in future is missing the valuable gift of present.
- Obsession with past and anxiety about future undermines the beauty of present.
- All the riches cannot retrieve the past. So live every moment of the present without unduly worrying about future.
- However glorious the past may be it is always the present which matters.
- Regretting the past and worrying about future is inimical whereas acting in the present buries your past, enlivens your present and secures your future.
- Living in the present and preparing for the future should be your motive rather than ruing the past.

PROBLEM

- Nature endows degree of capacity commensurate with the degree of problem. Break your problems into manageable pieces.
- Problems are an inferno which will either burn or purify you.
- Problems come to wake you up to realize your true potential.

- Treat everyone's problem as your own and you will be richly rewarded.
- All intractable problems can be solved when we act with a sense of purpose and humility.
- Think dispassionately about your problem as if its someone else's problem and you will definitely find a solution.
- Taking oneself too seriously is the crux of the problem.
- Problems need to be dealt with alacrity as they snowball into a Frankenstein.
- Problems can be solved if you analyze everything dispassionately and rationally.
- Every problem solved strengthens you.
- Problems are a boon to a person who accepts the challenge.
- Keep yourself involved in the problem of others and your problems will wane away.
- You are not alone in this world with intractable problems as you will realize that many people are beset with even more grave problems.
- Problems come to those who have the capacity to solve them.
- Without problems life will become insipid.
- All progress has its seed in problems.
- Never let problems seize your thinking. Instead embrace it as it will provide you valuable knowledge.
- Solution to your problems lie in solving problems of others.
- Most of our problems are imaginative with no basis.

PROGRESS

- Science needs to do away with destruction and religion with superstition.
- Your progress is directly proportional to your humility and inversely to ego.
- Road to progress is ridden with lot of trials and tribulations ultimately leading to triumph.

PROSPERITY

- Share your wealth, knowledge and happiness with others for true prosperity.
- Add at least one friend a day and you will ensure your prosperity.
- Glory and fame are a mirage if you chase them and they will chase you if you neglect them.
- Waiting for a favourable and opportune time to do great things is a mirage.
- Pursuit of gold is but a mirage. Real happiness is not guaranteed by money.

PURPOSE

- Purpose is more important than goals and objectives.
- Purpose of life is to elevate yourself and those around you to the acme of potential.
- Life without purpose is a body without soul.
- Leaving an imprint in the sands of time should be the aim of all.

- Purpose in life is like oxygen to the body. Purpose of life is to achieve greatness by harnessing the society.
- Employing unethical means to achieve ethical purpose is permissible.
- A solitary decision to live a life of purpose will elevate your personality.
- Purpose of human life is to leave a legacy for the posterity.
- Having a purpose will keep you cheerful and happy.
- Having a worthwhile purpose of bettering the society will keep you in tremendous mood and perennial bliss.
- Miracles ensue when there is purpose and action.
- Every moment is a joy for a person with a purpose.
- Pursuit of wealth should only be incidental to selfless service to humanity.
- Even if you stake everything to fulfill your dreams, it is worth it.
- Highly talented people often flounder for want of purpose.
- Stay foolish if it suits your purpose and not otherwise.
- Purpose of life should be to grow wise and aid others to grow.
- To give shape to your destiny and purpose, shape your thoughts and actions to that end.
- Hankering after name, fame and fortune may look wonderful in the beginning but may leave you flustered in the long run.
- When you are excited about a purpose it will make you restless and enthusiastic.
- Working for a purpose is much better than working for a living which makes you a slave of money.

- Freedom from anxiety and worry can be achieved if you have a clear cut purpose in life and you are whole-heartedly committed to it.
- A purpose will hold people together while selfishness will create chasms.
- Unless there is a compelling purpose your life will not provide the momentum to achieve great feats.
- Having a purpose in life will always keep you so busy that you will have no time for regrets.
- Rendering services emanating from purpose is more valuable than with an expectation of rewards.
- Greed and lust leads to misery whereas purpose leads to your coveted goal.
- You be the harbinger of a new dawn by awakening others to the purpose of life.
- Working for a living is worthless but for a purpose is very worthwhile.
- Sum and substance of life is how positively you have improved the lives of other people.
- Meandering your way through the maze of life can be made interesting if you act with purpose.
- Walk alone if need be if others are not enthusiastic about your purpose as you are your best judge.
- If your purpose covers the entire gamut of humanity then you will have broadened your horizons and potential.
- You can eat and have the cake if your purpose is in alignment with the needs of the people.
- Prospects of a bright future is guaranteed if your purpose is to do selfless service to the humanity.
- True life is living a life of purpose.

- To achieve great things we need to have a purpose and resoluteness.
- Awakening the people to their true purpose in life is the greatest gift you give to them.
- Dreams can be turned into reality if you have selfless purpose.
- Working for a purpose will lead you to your destiny rather than working for money and worldly things.
- Your purpose in life is to be of purpose to the society.
- World is replete with men of erudition who live miserable lives for want of purpose.
- Unless you have a purpose in life you are lost and you will just have a vegetable existence.
- Your purpose in life should align with that of impacting the lives of people in a positive way.
- In spite of all the problems purpose will put you on path to happiness.
- Your tryst with destiny will come if you live with purpose.

PURSUIT

- You will always find what you are looking for.
- Flowing like a river garnering everything on the way and merging with the ocean of divinity is all human life is about.

RAT RACE

- Indulging in the 'rat race' will make your life stressful.
- Don't be drawn into a rat race by copying others.
- Rat race is the biggest bane of human race.

- We are involuntarily dragged into rat race rather than living life on our own terms.

READING

- Reading good material daily will burgeon your wisdom to enable you to live a full blown life.
- Pleasure you derive by reading a worthwhile book is beyond any pleasure in the world.
- Reading books will enable you to unravel the world.
- The time spent on reading good books, ruminating about them and implementing them is highly commendable and rewarding.
- Though action is an antidote to many ills time spent on reading good books is really rewarding.
- Voracious readers never have boring moments.

REFORM

- Reform is better than punishment.
- Punitive measures have failed to transform humanity.
- We need to revamp the reform methods.
- Repenting for one's action is not enough unless remedial measures are taken.

REJUVENATION

- Periodically rejuvenating your personality will reap great rewards.

RELATION

- Treat your friends as brothers and brothers as your friends.

RELATIONSHIP

- Nourish every relationship lest they go into oblivion. Be tough on yourself and soft on others to fortify relationship.
- Keep nurturing your relationship with love to enjoy sublime life.
- Stubborn as a mule will destroy your relationship.
- Looking at opportunities to exploit your friends and relatives will strain your relationships.
- Pamper others and tamper self to fortify your personality.
- Relationships nurtured is a better asset than wealth.
- Nourish relationships, as that will enhance your happiness.
- Pursuit of wealth at the cost of relationships is futile.
- Don't take any relationship for granted as it requires perennial nurturing.
- Human relationships are more valuable than wealth.
- Money can ruin a relationship in a moment.
- Relationships should be nurtured gradually.
- Relationship is a ship of the desert coming to your rescue like a camel.
- Human relationships is the acme of all other considerations.
- Relationship based on trust, loyalty and empathy will withstand the ravages of time.
- Value human relationships more than wealth to have a purposeful life.

- Be childlike in matters of human relationships.
- Nurturing relationships is vital to long term relationships.
- Relationships are difficult to build and easy to break as they are as brittle as a glass.
- True friendship or relationship commands everything and never demands.
- Valuing relationships would stand in good stead in times of difficult times.
- Every relationship relies on trust and reciprocation.
- Never let intemperate behaviour spoil relationships.
- Most of the relationships become sour due to improper communication and lack of commitment.
- Don't treat any fight as the last as you may have to patch up with the same person.
- Develop relationship with all without expectations and you will enjoy your life.
- Relationships are as fragile and as fragrant as rose petals which need to be tended lovingly.
- Relationships are built on trust, love and continuity.
- Every relationship has the potential to provide you immense rewards provided you value and nourish them.
- Don't forget to nourish relationships in the hustle bustle of daily life as it is very vital to have relationships.
- Sink all the differences with your near and dear ones to have a congenial atmosphere.
- All relationships thrive when we overlook the faults and focus on the good qualities.
- Building a bond in relationship requires love, patience and sacrifice.

- Don't spit venom rather spit ambrosia as that would nourish relationships.
- We abruptly end our relationships little realizing there is lot of time for them to flourish.
- Relations flourish by constant nourishment. If you neglect or take it for granted then it will decay.
- Every relationship should not be weighed in terms of money as that would brand you as a mercenary.
- Don't rush at relationships but tread gingerly to allow opportunity to others to reciprocate.
- Social relations are more worthwhile than wealth and isolation.
- Value relationship like a tangible asset and it would turn out to be one.
- Relationship should be handled delicately lest they get soured and withered.
- Never bind a relationship with Gordian knots as that may denigrate.
- We realize the importance of relationships when we feel that our wealth stops to be of any use.

RELIGION

- Religion is a Frankenstein when it enters the public domain.
- Religions become archaic and an anachronism if not revamped to meet the needs of the time.
- A truly religious person will cast no harm to anyone.

- Religion is akin to science of the bygone days.
- Religion and superstition should not be abused to keep people in poverty.
- Spilling blood of human beings in the name of religion is most irreligious.
- Sacrilegious remarks against religion is acceptable but not blood-shedding in the name of religion.
- Religion's greatest challenge is to keep people away from sin and obdurateness.
- Spend time in worshipping the divinity but also find time to elevate the status of the ignorant and the poor.
- Killing in the name of religion is the most despicable thing.
- Religion should be a private affair and not public as when it becomes public it assumes fanaticism.
- No religion is greater than humanity.
- Religion, unless binds all human beings ceases to be of any significance.
- Religion should spread amity between entire humanity and if it is otherwise it needs to be done away with.
- Religion to be effective has to be free from ritualism and violence.

REPUTATION

- It takes quite a lot of time to build reputation but it can take a few moments to put it in shambles.
- Once you build a rocklike reputation, then you can command anything.

- Have a reputation like the rock of Gibraltar that it will remain solid even in the face of adversity.
- Reputation is like a fragile glass.
- Once your reputation is impaired it takes long to redeem that.

RESOLVE

- To remain aloof from the affairs of society requires great resolve.

RESPECT

- Respecting others motivates them and brings you respect. Treat everyone with respect and all the good will come to you.
- Treat everyone with the respect due to the greats.
- Respect for women, child and the old is a paragon of your culture.
- No one will respect you unless you respect yourself.
- Respect every individual in spite of his stature in the society.
- Treat every person with respect as he may be no more any moment.
- You need to deserve respect to get respect from others.
- If we do not respect our heritage and culture they will go into the oblivion.
- If you can secure the self-respect of others you will become a cynosure in the eyes of all.
- Do ventilate your feelings but do not hurt the feelings of others.

- Don't disparage lowly placed people as they are not to be blamed for their stature.
- Respect for others' views will make you respected by others.
- You are worthy of being called a true human if you respect everyone irrespective of their stature in society.
- However great you may be you cannot demand but only command respect.
- We must admire and respect the people who are constrained to do menial jobs for a living.
- Women, children and the old people need to be respected and cared for, for they deserve the most.
- Cringing from others is timidity and lack of self-respect.

RESPONSE

- Your response to a difficulty is more important than the event.
- Choose the response to every situation in a way it betters your life.

RESPONSIBILITY

- Blaming the stars for one's misfortune is avoiding responsibility.
- It is our responsibility towards posterity to stop plundering nature.
- We are as much free as we can be after we accept responsibility towards others.
- Dereliction of duty is born out of boredom and irresponsibility.

- We are ourselves responsible for our miseries as it is all in our perceptions of the world.
- Giving up on responsibility is akin to giving up life.
- Unless you discharge all your responsibilities you can not be free.
- The more you shy away from responsibility the more you suffer from the consequences of irresponsibility.
- Those who shirk responsibility cannot enjoy true freedom.
- Dreaming about freedom without responsibilities is a pipe dream.
- Skirting responsibility is a recipe for disaster.
- Taking responsibility for all your decisions and blaming none is a sign of highest maturity.
- Best way to relax is to discharge your responsibilities forthwith than procrastinating which precipitates the matter further.
- Dereliction of social responsibilities under the guise of spiritualism is an insult to life.
- Taking responsibility for oneself is good but for others is superb.

RESTRAINT

- Don't gloat over other's misfortunes as that is an invitation to your own misfortunes.

RUTHLESSNESS

- Personal tragedies are a frivolous thing for the ruthless world.
- Being practical is other word for ruthlessness.

RETICENCE

- To remain reticent is better than abusing others.

SANITY

- Only the threat from extra-terrestrial beings can bring back sanity to the world.
- No sane person will argue with the crowd as they are in a frenzy.

SEEK

- For want of seeking we may lose on something important.

SELF - CONTROL

- An unbridled tongue can be your nemesis.
- Best answer to nagging is keeping your mind and mouth shut.
- Freedom of speech is good as far as there is self-control over what you say.
- Refraining from criticism, complaining and condemning will reward you with beautiful things.

SELF

- Do adore your idols but also place yourself on a high pedestal.
- Self-condemnations are the worst disservice to oneself.
- Dialogue with your inner self is as paramount as having a dialogue with others.

- Keep stretching your limits as that would take you to unimaginable heights.
- Unless you try you will never fathom yourself.
- Thirst for praise makes you susceptible to exploitation.
- Push yourself to the extreme to increase your potential.
- Fool yourself to believe that you are confident and you will be.
- Be your own mentor to harness your potential.
- Focus on your own foibles rather than highlighting the faults of others.
- Keep digging into yourself to fathom your depth.
- Transform yourself before foraying into changing the world.
- Have a love affair with yourself before initiating with others.
- Keeping the demons within yourself at bay is more important than without.
- Harness your hidden talents to give your best to the society.
- Be a maverick in all what you do to create niche for yourself.
- Be as faithful as a dog and smart as a horse.
- Be polite to yourself to boost your morale.
- To enjoy one's own company requires tremendous determination.
- Don't spare yourself. Be tough on yourself and mild with others.

- Push yourself rather than beating about the bush.
- Awareness of self is awareness of the world.
- Being comfortable with oneself is necessary to make you comfortable with others.
- Self-praise works like tonic if sans arrogance.
- Self-admiration is an elixir to excel.
- Self-discovery reveals and manifests the true nature of world.
- Fathom yourself to fathom the world.
- Self-love is more desirable than self-pity.
- Turn your eyes inwards to cleanse yourself of faults.
- Your financial stature does not reflect your true worth.
- Triumph over self rewards you copiously.
- Channelize all your energy in improving yourself rather than dabbling in others' affairs.
- To unravel the mystery of life unravel yourself.
- Your true nature is unraveled when you are alone.
- You are your best help in times of crisis.
- Cooperate with yourself by not getting in your own way.
- Fathom your own self deeper and you will be amazed at your own potential.
- Much of the time we spend discussing the foibles of others we can spend it on self-improvement.
- Smooth or hurdle race you want is all in your hands.
- Making fun of yourself beckons the attention and goodwill of others.

- Spend every moment on self-improvement to enhance your personality.
- The amount of time we spend on criticizing, condemning and complaining can be better used to improve oneself.
- We ourselves commit the sins we accuse others of.
- Many blunders occur because we consider ourselves infallible.
- Opening the mouth for gormandizing and needless chatter is fraught with disaster.
- Understand yourself first rather than trying to understand others.
- Wonder and excitement keeps you charged up.
- Manage yourself and you can manage anything.
- Inner strength is so formidable that you hardly have to rely on others.
- Respecting yourself is also equally important when you are tempted to overdo to others.
- There is treasure hidden in ourselves if we believe.
- Fall in love with yourself head over heels and enjoy your own company and you will relate better with other people.
- Don't continue in the circumstances which are not close to your heart as it will be a drudgery to yourself and injustice to the employer.
- Be your own sculptor and remove the unwanted to shape yourself to perfection.
- Praising self also is essential to keep your morale high.
- Being ruthlessly strict with oneself is very rewarding but not with others.

- You know yourself better than others. So don't expect an excellence certificate from others.
- Don't permit anybody to set agenda for you as you are your best judge.
- Every problem and every solution is within you if you genuinely attempt.
- Your unhappiness has its roots in your mind and not outside.
- Pamper your humility and tamper your ego.
- Basking under your own glory is acceptable than regretting your weaknesses.
- You are yourself a magnificent, magical and miraculous machine that will do the wonders for you and the rest of the world.
- Working for oneself requires irresolute determination and responsibility as there is no one to egg on.
- Don't become a puppet in anybody's hands.
- Be your own decision-maker.
- Internal forces are more powerful than external ones.
- Conquest of self is the greatest triumph.
- The world inside is mightier than the world without.
- You be your own commander to fulfill your dream.
- Keep risking and keep challenging yourself to make yourself a colossus.
- One may fool others but cannot fool oneself.
- Don't ostracize yourself from the society from where you get all the gifts.

- You cannot love the world if you do not love yourself.
- Treat yourself with respect as that would attract respect from others.
- Laughing at oneself will give you more pleasure and secure more friends than laughing at others.
- The world looks at you the way you look at it.
- Everyone is a history and mystery unto himself.
- No body knows better your qualities, skills and potential than yourself.
- Be tough on yourself and soft on others.
- You sing the praises of the heroes little realizing that you are also a hero in your life.
- Once you realize that you yourself are capable of reaching great heights you will have won half the battle.
- Be in competition with yourself and in cooperation with others to live a peaceful and prosperous life.
- Anybody can rock your boat if you lack principles, character and scruples.

SELF-CONFIDENCE

- Self-confidence will extinguish all negative feelings of fear, doubt and anxiety. Enhance your self-confidence by self-affirmations of positive kind.
- Confidence in oneself is more important than clinging on to someone with aplomb.

SELF-ESTEEM

- Self-esteem is far better than a great award.
- Lack of self-esteem will demoralize you.
- Raise your esteem in your own eyes rather than expecting from others.
- Keep vices at bay as they may devastate you and put you in a quandary.

SELFISHNESS

- Selfishness is the unbecoming of a human being.
- Selfishness is the worst trait of human beings leading us to catastrophe.
- Don't get into the quagmire of selfishness.
- All the stress and tension is the outcome of selfishness.
- Organizations and persons striving only to serve their ends are a slur on humanity.
- Selfishness is at the root of all evils.

SELFLESSNESS

- Rejoicing and celebrating the happiness of others will keep you on a high.

SELF-LOVE

- Self-love is the beginning of loving others.
- Love for others emanates from self-love.

SERVICE

- Duty has negative connotations so involvement for service is a better word.
- Keep your focus on the goals that are in line with the service to others. That would certainly bring rich rewards.
- Making wealth should be incidental to serving the society and not an endeavor for itself.

SHADOWS

- Shadows of your deeds will never leave you.

SHARING

- Sharing your riches and love will make your life an eternal bliss.
- If everyone shares his riches with the have-nots then there would be no misery.
- Share your knowledge, happiness and riches with others and it multiplies and sharing your concerns, fears and grieves with others will divide it.

SIMPLICITY

- Keeping your life simple will keep you happy and away from petulance.
- Simplicity is more complex than complexity itself.
- Simplicity is humility par excellence.
- Simplify your life to avert stress.
- Be simple but avoid falling into the trap of charlatans.

SIN

- It is the worst sin to snatch the bread of a poor man.
- We must break the bones of the sinister people and feed it to the vultures.
- Sin against the very person who helped you in times of need is the worst treachery.
- It is the greatest sin to know the gravity and not warn.

SKILL

- To acquire the right kind of knowledge is a vital skill.
- Candor coupled with tact is the best communication skill you can possess.
- Maximize your potential by harnessing what skills you are good at rather than trying to dabble with what you don't have.

SKIRMISHES

- Time lost on skirmishes is irretrievable.
- Don't engage in skirmishes over trivial things.
- Little skirmishes lead to serious altercation if blended with adamancy on both sides.

SMILE

- A simple smile can countenance any enmity.
- Smile even at strangers and you will benefit immensely.
- Smile sends friendly vibes to others.
- An effortless smile has tremendous face value.

- Smile costs nothing but gains everything.
- Smile is the best cosmetic endowed to human beings.
- Dissolve all hurdles with a lavish smile.
- Smile emanates from a happy heart and sends a signal of friendship.
- Keep smiling in dire circumstances to drive away the effect of misery.
- Welcome all the situation with a smile on your face and you will have no regrets.
- A genuine smile disarms all hostility and wins friends.
- A simple smile can make most hostile situation into a friendly one.
- Smiling is very contagious so is anger but with disastrous results.
- A genuine and broad smile on your face is the passport to any place.
- However depressed put up a face with a smile and everything will vanish for good.
- A genuine smile can disarm the worst enemy.
- Smile is a good wear to put on rather than costly attire.
- A genuine smile is the greatest asset in your repertoire.
- Smile dissolves all enmity and adversity.
- Look for reasons to smile rather than grieve and you will be perpetually happy.
- A smiling face is the cynosure of all people.
- Keep smiling even in the face of calamity as it drives away misfortune.
- Smile is like sunshine which drives away all misfortunes.
- Smiles bring out the best in others and frown the worst.

SOCIETY

- Every dime you spend should benefit the whole society.
- Our treatment of human beings as a commodity has rendered the society in shambles.
- Commit yourself to the good of the society and your own dreams will be fulfilled.
- Looking beyond yourself and your family is vital for the growth of self and society.
- A blend of tradition sans superstition and modernity sans avarice is required to create a prosperous and progressive world society.
- Societal pressure to fall in line should be challenged and new paradigm should be adopted.
- Integration of old generation and the younger generation is paramount to having a salubrious society.

SOLACE

- Commiserate with the affected to bring solace to them.
- Wipe the tears of others and bring cheers to them. That is the best help you can provide.

SOLITUDE

- Solitude empowers you greatly to introspect.
- Solitude is never inimical to a wise man.

SOLUTION

- Look into yourself for solution to all your problems.
- Solution to tackle uncertainty is to plan and take positive action with no anxiety.

- You get paid not for solving your own problem but for solving the problems of others.

SPEECH

- Unbridled tongue breaks many a relationships.
- Your speech should be mellifluous as that would make the other person comfortable.
- Speak your mind when you ought to as you will never have a second chance.
- Your talk should unravel your character and not conceal it.
- Be brief in what you say as that may save you tons of heartburns.
- Listen very carefully before you start speaking.

SPIRITUALITY

- Pleasure from material things fizzles out sooner than later but that of spiritual kind lasts for time immemorial.
- Spirituality has the potential to achieve the utopian dream of paradise on earth.
- Mystery shrouding spirituality can be unveiled by understanding each other.

STRENGTH

- Keep focusing on your strengths as that would make you formidable. Every problem vanquished enhances your strength.
- Embrace every problem with cheer and you will grow in strength.
- You are as strong as your weakest habits.

- Your formidable strength of resilience is revealed when faced with adversity.
- Forgiveness must emanate from strength and not weakness.
- Friend and foe are alike in the sense both make you strong.
- Everything should be a source of strength.

STUBBORNNESS

- Stubborn as a mule only affects that person.

STUCK

- Falling in a quagmire is alright but staying there is bad.

SUCCESS

- Success is coming unscathed through an odyssey of failures.
- Success is guaranteed if words and deeds synchronize.
- True success is when everyone involved is happy.
- Success is springing back to life with resilience from failure.
- Treat failure with scant respect and proceed towards your coveted goal.
- Living up to your own expectations is real success as living up to that of others is conceding defeat.
- Success is a failure if it alienates you from your near and dear ones.
- Failure is a success if you befriend all the people you come in contact with.
- Failure is not an anathema but an evidence of the attempt to succeed.

- There may be thousand faults in you but one good talent is enough to succeed in life.
- Decide the best thing you love to do and focus all your energies on that and you will be astounded by the results.
- Put in all you can in terms of efforts, commitment and enthusiasm and have no anxiety and you will surely succeed.
- While seeking something superb leave scope for failure as it may leave you unaffected.
- Unless you go through a series of failures success will not ensue.
- Tryst with triumph comes to those who keep on getting up every time they stumble.
- Failure is as sweet as success when what you have tried is humongous.
- Act as if nothing is going to fail and think as if everything is going to succeed.
- True success is in shaping your life around your heart's desire and not by the agenda of others.
- Success if not digested leads to arrogance which is inimical to your growth.
- Mobilize, motivate and manage all your resources to attain acme of success.
- Adroitness coupled with attitude and enthusiasm is vital for success.
- If the success makes you arrogant then it is not a true success.
- If you have wisdom and humility in your repertoire you will win all the games.
- Doing things by fits and starts is the sure shot way to mar the prospects of success.

- If you can provide what people want then your success is guaranteed.
- For every success preparation is required.
- Keep pursuing things with enthusiasm and hope and you will certainly succeed.
- Create your own success mantra as that has better chance of success.
- Keep taking actions without anxiety of expectation and you will succeed in everything.
- Failure is just a milestone on way to success.
- Consciously thinking those thoughts which are beneficial is vital to success.
- Success can best be measured in terms of relationships you have built and the number of lives bettered.
- Success can make you drunk with ego if you are not humble in your victory.
- Real success and happiness comes from how many hearts you have won and not how many fortresses.
- Taking all the roadblocks and hurdles in your stride is necessary to achieve true success.
- Mentors and coaches make your journey to success easier as doing it on your own may be frustrating.
- Debacles are the pathway to grand success if taken in proper perspective.

TEMPERAMENT

- Having an ice-berg temperament will make you a rock-like personality.
- Cool as cucumber will remove all encumbers.
- You are your own nemesis if you are dogmatic.

- Sign of maturity is being sangfroid in any situation.
- Keeping your cool even in times of crisis will immensely help.
- A cool temperament is a sign of great maturity.
- Temperament is far important than skill.
- An intemperate person is a difficult person to get along with.
- Nothing is beyond the reach of a person who is discerning and cool.
- Getting irritated at petty things is a poor reflection of your temperament.
- Develop temperament to tackle adversities.
- However grave the provocation may be keeping your cool will resolve the issue.
- Losing temper and patience is a sign of ignorance and arrogance.
- A cool head can achieve anything.
- Cool, calm and composed cures crisis.
- Cool temperament will save you lot of headaches.

TEMPTATION

- Temptation within bounds is good for you.
- Avoid the temptation to say something unwarranted.
- Don't yield to the temptation to adopt short-cuts to prosperity as it may turn into tragedy.
- We need to resist the temptation to tear someone into smithereens as most of the times it boomerangs.
- We must overcome temptations to emulate the venal people which may look the most easiest and simplest way to riches.

- Some temptations are such that they require tremendous will power to resist them.
- Gazing at beauty is thrilling provided you don't fall prey to the temptation to possess it.
- We are tempted to say something on a subject we are ignorant just to impress others.
- It is easier to fall prey to temptations than standing by principles.
- Whenever you forego a temptation you have strengthened yourself.
- It is more difficult to resist a temptation than falling prey to it.
- Temptation to say something should be avoided as that might land you in trouble.
- Replete are the temptations to transgress but your conscience will guide you to ward them off.
- World is full of temptations luring you to get ensnared but you should resolutely endeavor to avoid them.

TENSION

- Tension and strife lead to frustration.

THINKING

- Keep the doors closed for negative thinking.
- Unbiased thinking can give you a lot of clarity.
- Regimented thinking leaves no room for new ideas which may prove to be pernicious for you.
- Always think of ways to get out from the status quo and achieve a niche for yourself.

- Any affliction of body and mind is the outcome of our thinking.
- Always thinking about negative things brings about the negatives.
- A dwarf may be a colossus by his thinking and a colossus may be a dwarf by his thinking.
- Trial and error method is beset with many problems which can be solved by thinking with clarity.
- Profound thinking coupled with positive attitude and action will aid in achieving great feats.
- Come out of your dwarf thinking and become a giant.

THIRST

- Quenching the thirst for material things will render you unhappy whereas that for wisdom will be most enriching.
- Quench the thirst for knowledge and wisdom rather than materialistic gains.

THOUGHTS

- Keep trimming your thoughts lest they grow into a monster. Flush your negative thoughts and nurture positive thoughts.
- Drive away negative thoughts from your mind and shelter positive thoughts.
- Nurture only good thoughts in your mind to reap rich dividends.
- Thoughts if unchecked can ruin your personality.
- Quality of life depends on quality of thoughts.
- Watch every thought before you turn into action.

- Banish all negative thoughts and fill your mind with positive thoughts to attain glory.
- Rein in your thoughts and your life will transform .
- A person in prison may have the feeling of freedom if his thoughts are positive and a person enjoying freedom may feel incarcerated if his thoughts are negative.
- Quell a negative thought by replacing it with a positive thought.
- Keeping vigil over your thoughts is absolutely vital as your mind wanders aimlessly.
- Thinking negative thoughts sags your morale and thinking positive thoughts raises you to ecstasy.
- Negative thoughts needlessly hamper your progress.
- Ruminating negative thoughts lead to continual misery.
- Nourish your brain with happy thoughts and you will flourish.
- A profusion of positive thoughts should be encouraged as it has all the potential to make you great.
- Thinking positive thoughts is the most inexpensive albeit luxurious activity.
- Thoughts of the past are dinosaurs which need to be driven away to leave room for new thoughts.
- Play acrobatics with your thoughts and you will enjoy every moment.
- Monitoring your thoughts will monitor your action and your action will determine your destiny.
- Wonderful thoughts lead you to wonderful beliefs, wonderful dreams and wonderful life.
- In the moment of unhappiness switch your mind to happy thoughts and you will be happy again.

- Open the floodgates of thoughts and channelize your thoughts in the direction of your dreams.
- Monitoring thoughts and channelizing them into shaping your destiny is a worthwhile task.
- It's the quality of thought that makes one a genius or an ignoramus.
- Screen your thoughts and do not allow negative thoughts to enter your mind as that would make your life miserable.
- Thoughts are also tangible things as they are the foundation for all the castles we build.
- Shaping your thoughts will shape your destiny.
- Killing boredom is easy if you initiate free-flowing thoughts.
- Treat every good thought as a gem and you will become a gem.

TIME

- Time is irretrievable, so enjoy and relish every moment.
- Look for ways to build your personality and do not squander your valuable time in gossiping .
- Don't leave scope for repentance for having squandered precious moments.
- Time trickles so fast, by the time you realize, it has flown away.
- Spend invaluable time in propping up your personality rather than on finding fault with others.
- Every second should be relished as pearls and not pebbles.
- Never waste your time on petty things as you would get entangled in the cobweb of ordinary.

- One life time is not enough to assimilate all the knowledge and wisdom and it is tragic that we while away our time in trivial matters.
- Time is a resource which gets spent any way even if you do not spend it.
- Time doesn't pass we pass through time.
- Time is a wealth nobody can buy.

TITHING

- Tithing should be a regular affair to express gratitude for the gift of life.

TREACHERY

- Treachery is the worst form of inhumanity.
- We despise the very people who provide us with all the goodies in our lives.
- Seeking prosperity by unethical means is a treachery against society.
- Modern day leaders have become the neo-monarchs usurping all the power of the common man.
- Never leave those in the lurch who are relying on you for their survival.
- Never accuse anyone of treachery as most of the times it is our own fault to trust people easily.
- Ditching your friends and parents for money is treachery of the highest order.
- Never leave anyone in the lurch after raising his hopes as it serves no purpose but impairs your credibility.

TREASURE

- Deep within you lies the treasure which you need to discover.
- Treasure the moments of joy and bury the nightmares.
- You have everything within you to garner all the things you want out of life.
- Bring the best from the closet of your mind to shine splendidly.
- Mélange of skills are hidden in you. You just need to discover and harness them to your and everyone's benefit.
- All the treasure is buried in your subconscious mind. So explore the potential of your subconscious.

TRIALS

- Trials and tribulations test your mettle and fortify your personality.
- Trials, tribulations and adversities will make you either defeated or triumphant.

TROUBLE

- Never stir a hornet's nest as you would be needlessly inviting trouble.
- Avoid trouble as that is worse than poison.

TRUE SUCCESS

- Fulfill the needs of others and your own needs will be fulfilled.

TRUST

- Trust works better than stick.
- Trust has to be commanded and not demanded.
- If you mistrust yourself you will not trust anybody.
- Relying on others to deliver requires relinquishing supervision.
- Trust needs to be reposed only after checking and double checking as any hasty decision will make you repent in future.
- It is better to get betrayed than mistrusting someone.
- Never trust your eyes rather trust your heart.

TRUTH

- Truth may be at variance with your belief.
- Quest for truth starts from probing oneself deeply.
- Sugar coated truths are better than truth dispensed with harshness, as it is soft like a petal on the receiver.
- When in doubt, question the wise to understand the truth.
- Every written word should not be treated as gospel truth as they may have been written to hoodwink the gullible masses.
- Telling the truth makes you formidable.

UNDERSTANDING

- Take time to understand others as that would pay rich dividends.
- Understanding oneself should precede understanding of others.

- Take time to understand yourself and as well as others.
- Conundrum of life can be resolved by understanding oneself thoroughly.
- Travelling should be used to enhance your understanding of the people, places and culture and not to boast to your friends.

UNETHICAL

- Unethical means to achieve your goals is debauchery.

VALUES

- We need to redeem the vestiges of humanitarian values.
- Science may advance by leaps and bounds but human values will be for eternity.
- Fishing in troubled waters is an assault on human values.
- We do not value the things till we lose the same.
- Intrinsic worth is more valuable than face value as beauty without brain is of no value.

VICES

- Don't keep company with vices as that would transform you into a devil.
- Befriending vices is having inimical enemy.
- Squandering money on vices is the greatest blunder.
- Even a solitary vice can spell doom for you.
- It is better to be idle than to indulge in vices.

- Blind pursuit of wine, women and wealth is the surest way to our nemesis.
- Keep vices at an arm's length as it's shadow is also potent with peril.
- Don't dabble with vices as they may become your foe.
- Keep yourself judiciously out of vices which may lead you to your nemesis.
- Tinkering with vices is a recipe for disaster.
- Vices are honey tempered with poison.
- Pursuit of wine, women and wealth may look thrilling but are killing.

VICIOUS CIRCLE

- Ignorance leads to anger and anger leads to crime.

VIRTUE

- Vulgarity is being worshiped as a virtue in recent times.
- Be the paragon of virtues to reap bliss.
- Extolling the virtues of others is good but it will be better to develop virtues ourselves.
- Be a beacon of virtues to enable others to see the light.
- Having character and courage in your repertoire is the best weapon.
- Confluence of knowledge and integrity is the best blend.
- Be like a horse in speed and smartness and a donkey for carrying the necessary burden.
- Remaining calm under trying circumstances is the virtue of the great.

- Develop virtues as that would immensely increase your personality.
- Cultivating virtues is immensely a tough task but once acquired they will be an asset.
- Knowledge coupled with humility is a rare virtue deserving accolades.
- Expecting in return for your virtues is not correct rather they are rewards by themselves.

VISUALIZATION

- Visualize everything before you commence any work as that would immensely enhance your efficiency.
- Visualize the consequences before taking any action.
- Loneliness can be enriched if you get into the mood of creative visualization.

WANTS

- Limit your wants and you will be happy beyond measures.

WAR

- However lofty the ideals may be, to wage war is unprincipled.
- War emanates from unsatisfied souls and avarice.

WEALTH

- Making a living only for garnering wealth is tantamount to prostitution. Using religion towards garnering wealth is debauchery.

- Pursuit of wealth should not make you a mercenary.
- The time spent on amassing wealth is useful only if you are able to enjoy that wealth.
- Don't be drunk with the intoxication of wealth as it may evaporate any moment.
- Wealth beyond proportions ostracizes you from many people.
- You can fake anything but not wealth.

WILL

- There is no dearth of opportunities for a willing person.
- Torrents of defeats cannot trample a person with iron will.

WISDOM

- Use wisdom as your guide and you will relish every moment.

  A wise man will take every thing in his stride without a whimper of protest.
- Knowledge tempered with wisdom will elevate you and make you feel ecstatic.
- Ignorance leads to arrogance and wisdom leads to humility.
- Leaving behind a legacy of wisdom is far more valuable than all the valuables.
- Every mistake is a learning experience to be turned into wisdom.
- Wisdom is universal and has no boundaries of country and religion.

- No amount of wealth is enough in the pursuit of knowledge and wisdom.
- Wisdom is like seasoned wine.
- For the wise loss of words is far worse than loss of money.
- Wisdom is the ambrosia of the greats.
- Foolishness born out of wisdom is much adorable thing than intelligence born out of arrogance.
- Sift the chaff of trash from the information overload.
- Wisdom is worth more than all the formal degrees.
- Ancient wisdom is enough to run the world.
- Quench the thirst for wisdom.
- Wisdom is the key to true happiness.
- Wealth without wisdom is cataclysmic.
- Keep your mind open to all wisdom to achieve greatness.
- Be proud of your wisdom rather than of wealth.
- Wisdom lies in reining in your ego, anger and arrogance.
- Wisdom lies in keeping silent by avoiding the temptation to speak.
- Disseminate knowledge and wisdom to dispel the darkness from the world.
- Ravages of time will leave everything in tatters except wisdom.
- Knowledge and wisdom can be shared with all in abundance keeping the treasure trove intact.
- The intoxication from the opium of wisdom is worthwhile.
- Seek wisdom and not evanescent things.

- Gift of wisdom is better than monetary gift.
- Wisdom is the fountain head of joy and bliss.
- Wisdom gives you purpose in life.
- Pursuit of wisdom will give you proper perspective of life.
- Garnering wisdom will provide you with immense happiness rather than the rat race for wealth which compels you to stress yourself to the point of discomfiture.
- Seek wisdom to make your life meaningful and enriching.
- A pearl of wisdom is better than a voluminous harangue.
- Having wisdom will obviate apathy.
- We can always find solace in wisdom of the yore in times of crisis.
- Labyrinth of life can be better understood through wisdom.
- Fragrance of wisdom wafts to every corner.
- Men of erudition seldom indulge in murky things.
- Fragrance of wisdom pervades the whole world.
- Acquire the wisdom that will guide in your quest for truth.
- If wisdom prevails, then everything is hunky dory.
- Kernel of wisdom is at the heart of the fruit of knowledge.
- Abundance of wealth is often a dampener to understand the wisdom of the world.
- Bathe your mind with wisdom everyday to keep it clean and fresh.
- Except wisdom everything else is ephemeral. So embrace the eternal.
- Give a stiff dose of wisdom to yourself to raise your level of awareness.

- Gobble up all the wisdom and make it an integral part of your personality.
- Spread wisdom and love to all who come in contact with you to make this world a better place to live.
- Wisdom may lead to wealth but wealth may not lead to wisdom.
- Seek wisdom and wisdom will yield abundance in all respects.
- Gems of wisdom are much more precious than material gems as they have the potential to shower abundance on you.
- Exploring the world to understand and seek wisdom is a worthy pursuit.
- Wisdom will overpower beauty which is ephemeral.
- Wisdom is not the exclusive preserve of the erudite as even an illiterate may have that.
- Wealth when shared dwindles whereas wisdom grows with sharing.
- Waning with age may afflict your body and not your wisdom.
- Pretending ignorance at opportune times is also a kind of wisdom which saves the situation turning into a disaster.
- Wisdom is an opium elevating you to great heights and ecstasy.
- The exuberance wisdom gives is unmatched by any other pleasure.
- Wisdom sans humility is arrogance of the worst kind.
- Looking sheepish is good when illiterates are blabbering.
- Wisdom is distilled knowledge emanating from difficult experiences.

- Pearls of wisdom are better than pearls of gems.
- Road to wisdom is very tough but once you reach there you have landed in paradise.
- Vintage wisdom is like vintage wine which gives subtle pleasure.
- Wisdom will make you humble and affable.
- Growing old physically has no sense and commands no respect unless coupled with wisdom.
- It takes one wise man to change the world.
- Wisdom is a magic wand which can achieve incredible things.
- Pursuing wisdom is a worthwhile pursuit in exclusion to other things.
- Education can teach you only to read, write and speak but it is wisdom which can make you understand.
- Gobbling up wisdom will give you a lot of pleasure and will be very rewarding.

WORK

- Work should be fun and not torture.
- Respect work as an opportunity to ameliorate the lives of others.
- Treat every job with respect as even a menial one will reward you richly.
- Too much of work will ruin health and relationships and too much of relaxation leads to decay.

- Work unless treated as joy and fun tends to become monotonous and an albatross.
- Treat your work as worship and you will fully exploit your latent talents.
- Life's meaning is to work ceaselessly to create a better world.
- If you cannot find joy and fun in your work then it becomes boring and routine.
- Doing your work with gusto will make you happy.
- Never mock at any work even if it is menial as destiny may mock at you.
- Work shapes man and man shapes work.
- If hard work were to pay then donkeys would have flourished.
- Work sans fun becomes a drudgery.

WORLD

- Heaven and hell are all on the terra firma.
- The world ruthlessly carries on caring less for the tragedy and misfortune that befalls on mankind.
- Only inimical threat to the world will awaken the people from comatose.
- World is an arena where everyone has a role to play.
- The world is so ruthless that it will try to put obstacles in your chosen path.
- The whole world is a mirage as you are clamouring for more or more.

- The more you chase something the more it turns out to be an unreal thing.
- The world cannot be the fiefdom of the richest as it equally belongs to the poorest.
- The world belongs collectively to all and individually to none.

WORRY

- Worry is a dwarf monster which can grow into a Frankenstein if not tackled.
- Worry leads you nowhere but thinking certainly.
- Worry is a gruesome ghost which torments you to no end and jeopardizes your clarity of thoughts.
- Worry plays havoc with your psyche and hope enlivens you.
- Excessively worrying about the future will mar the present.
- Worrying profusely about results spoils the joy of efforts.
- Always worrying about your own problems is the recipe for misery.
- Worrying is a flame which burns your energy resulting in wastage and frustration.

WORTH

- To a famished person even stale food is relishing.
- Sift the worthy from the clutter to be of use to you.
- Don't count anybody's worth by his wealth rather do that by his contribution to the society.

- Doing good deeds with an eye on rewards and accolades is not worthwhile.
- Intrinsic worth is far better than the face value as it is the genuine thing.

QUALITY

- Quality of life is preferable over quantity.
- Sculpturing your personality into greatness depends on the quality of your thoughts and action.

ZEST

- Zest for life is enough to make for the deficit in talent.
- Zest for life will make you relish every moment however good or bad it might be.
- If you have no zest for life than you are missing one of the best virtues of life.